The DevOps Journey: Navigating the Path to Seamless Software Delivery

Kameron Hussain

Published by Sonar Publishing, 2024.

THE DEVOPS JOURNEY: NAVIGATING THE PATH TO SEAMLESS SOFTWARE DELIVERY

First edition. March 10, 2024.

Copyright © 2024 Kameron Hussain.

ISBN: 979-8224328840

Written by Kameron Hussain.

Table of Contents

DevOps Approach

Contrasting Outcomes

1.5 Key Benefits of Adopting DevOps

1. Improved Collaboration

2. Faster Time-to-Market

3. Increased Reliability

4. Enhanced Quality

5. Cost Efficiency

6. Agility and Adaptability

7. Continuous Feedback and Improvement

8. Scalability

9. Competitive Advantage

10. Risk Mitigation

Chapter 2: DevOps Culture and Mindset

2.1 Building a DevOps Culture: Collaboration and Communication

Collaboration Across Silos

Communication and Transparency

Cross-Training and Skill Sharing

Empowering Teams

Best Practices for CI Setup

Example CI Configuration (Jenkinsfile)

4.3 Best Practices for Continuous Deployment

1. Automate Everything

2. Implement Continuous Integration First

3. Small, Frequent Releases

4. Blue-Green Deployments

5. Rollback Plans

6. Feature Flags and Toggles

7. Immutable Infrastructure

8. Automated Testing at All Stages

9. Monitoring and Alerts

10. Security as Code

11. Documentation and Runbooks

12. Collaboration and Communication

13. Testing in Production

14. Immutable Artifact Repositories

15. Continuous Feedback and Improvement

16. Disaster Recovery Plans

17. Compliance and Auditing

10.2 Orchestration with Kubernetes

Key Concepts in Kubernetes

Why Use Kubernetes?

Setting Up a Kubernetes Cluster

10.3 Containerization Best Practices

1. Single Responsibility Principle:

2. Immutable Containers:

3. Version Tagging:

4. Minimal Base Images:

5. Environment Configuration:

6. Secrets Management:

7. Health Checks:

8. Container Scanning:

9. Resource Limits:

10. Logging and Monitoring:

11. Container Orchestration:

12. Distributed Tracing:

13. Caching and State Management:

14. Testing:

15. Documentation:

16. Backup and Disaster Recovery:

17. Container Registry Security:

18. Continuous Integration/Continuous Deployment (CI/CD):

19. Networking:

20. Education and Training:

10.4 Microservices and Containers

Microservices Architecture:

Advantages of Microservices:

Containerization and Microservices:

Challenges:

Best Practices:

10.5 Managing Stateful and Stateless Applications

Stateful Applications:

Stateless Applications:

Managing Stateful Applications in Containers:

Managing Stateless Applications in Containers:

Chapter 11: Microservices and DevOps

Section 11.1: Understanding Microservices Architecture

Section 11.2: Aligning Microservices with DevOps Principles

Section 11.3: Challenges in Microservices Deployment

Section 11.4: Monitoring and Managing Microservices

Section 11.5: Case Studies: Transitioning to Microservices

Chapter 11: Microservices and DevOps

Section 11.1: Understanding Microservices Architecture

Section 11.2: Aligning Microservices with DevOps Principles

Section 11.3: Challenges in Microservices Deployment

1. Service Discovery and Communication

2. Data Management

3. Deployment Automation

4. Service Dependencies

5. Monitoring and Debugging

6. Security

7. Versioning and Compatibility

8. Scalability

9. Organizational Culture

10. Testing

Section 11.4: Monitoring and Managing Microservices

1. Real-Time Monitoring

2. Distributed Tracing

3. Centralized Logging

4. Alerting and Notification

5. Auto-Scaling

6. Load Balancing

7. Service Mesh

8. Performance Testing

9. Security Monitoring

10. Capacity Planning

11. Continuous Improvement

12. Chaos Engineering

Section 11.5: Case Studies: Transitioning to Microservices

1. Netflix

2. Amazon

3. Uber

4. Airbnb

5. Spotify

Chapter 12: Scaling DevOps Practices

Section 12.1: Strategies for Scaling DevOps in Large Organizations

Section 12.5: Success Stories of DevOps at Scale

1. Netflix

2. Amazon Web Services (AWS)

3. Target

4. Microsoft

5. Capital One

6. Google

7. Etsy

8. Facebook

Section 13.1: Key Performance Indicators in DevOps

1. Deployment Frequency

2. Lead Time for Changes

3. Change Failure Rate

4. Mean Time to Recovery (MTTR)

5. Availability and Reliability

6. Customer Satisfaction

7. Code Quality Metrics

8. Infrastructure Utilization

9. Work in Progress (WIP)

10. DevOps Culture Metrics

Case Studies

Challenges

Section 19.5: Future Prospects of DevOps Worldwide

1. Expansion Across Industries

2. DevOps in Small and Medium Enterprises (SMEs)

3. The Role of Artificial Intelligence (AI)

4. Serverless and Edge Computing

5. Enhanced Security Integration

6. Cross-Platform and Multi-Cloud Deployments

7. Regulatory Compliance and Governance

8. Continuous Learning and Certification

9. Global Collaboration

10. Sustainability and Green DevOps

Chapter 20: Preparing for the Future of DevOps

Section 20.1: Emerging Technologies and Trends in DevOps

1. GitOps

2. Progressive Delivery

3. Infrastructure as Code (IaC) Evolution

4. AIOps (Artificial Intelligence for IT Operations)

Continuous Integration and Deployment (CI/CD) for Edge Applications

Monitoring and Management of Edge Devices

Edge Security and DevSecOps

Scaling Edge Deployments

Edge and Cloud Integration

Edge DevOps Best Practices

Section 20.4: Preparing for the Next Wave of DevOps Innovations

1. GitOps and Infrastructure as Code (IaC) Maturation

2. AIOps and Intelligent Automation

3. Serverless and Function as a Service (FaaS)

4. Edge DevOps and Edge-native Applications

5. DevOps for AI and Machine Learning (MLOps)

6. Cloud-native and Kubernetes-native DevOps

7. Quantum Computing DevOps

8. Regulatory and Compliance Automation

9. DevOps for Non-Traditional IT Environments

10. Ethical DevOps and Responsible AI

Section 20.5: Envisioning the Future of Software Development with DevOps

1. DevOps as the New Standard

2. AI-Augmented Development

3. No-Code and Low-Code Development

4. Cloud-Native and Hybrid Architectures

5. Decentralized and Distributed Teams

6. Continuous Everything

7. DevOps for IoT and Edge Computing

8. Enhanced Security Integration

9. User-Centric Development

10. Sustainable and Responsible Development

Chapter 1: Understanding DevOps

1.1 The Evolution of Software Development

Software development has undergone a significant evolution over the years, shaped by technological advancements, changing business demands, and the need for more efficient and agile processes. This evolution has ultimately led to the emergence of DevOps as a critical approach to software engineering.

In the early days of software development, the Waterfall model was the predominant methodology. This linear and sequential approach involved distinct phases such as requirements gathering, design, development, testing, and deployment, with each phase tightly coupled to the next. While it provided structure, Waterfall often resulted in lengthy development cycles and limited collaboration between different teams.

With the advent of Agile methodologies in the late 20th century, software development started to shift towards a more iterative and collaborative approach. Agile emphasized customer feedback, adaptability, and cross-functional teams, allowing for faster releases and greater customer satisfaction. However, even Agile had limitations when it came to addressing the gap between development and operations.

This gap became more pronounced as software systems grew in complexity, and the need for frequent and reliable deployments increased. Traditional IT practices were often siloed, with development teams focusing solely on writing code, while operations teams were responsible for infrastructure and deployment. This disconnect between development and operations gave rise to inefficiencies, communication bottlenecks, and delayed software delivery.

The need to bridge this gap and create a seamless software delivery pipeline led to the evolution of DevOps. DevOps, a portmanteau of "Development" and "Operations," emerged as a cultural and technical movement that aimed to break down silos, foster collaboration, and automate repetitive tasks throughout the software delivery lifecycle.

At its core, DevOps is about aligning the goals of development and operations teams to achieve faster, more reliable, and continuous delivery of software. It promotes a cultural shift where communication, collaboration, and shared responsibilities become integral to the development process. In addition to cultural changes, DevOps leverages automation, version control, and various tools to streamline processes, enhance quality, and enable rapid deployments.

DevOps represents a departure from traditional, rigid software development practices and embraces a more dynamic and customer-centric approach. It acknowledges that software is never static, and it encourages continuous improvement, learning, and adaptation to meet evolving business needs.

In summary, the evolution of software development has led to the emergence of DevOps as a transformative approach that addresses the challenges of modern software engineering. DevOps seeks to bridge the gap between development and operations, fostering collaboration, automation, and agility throughout the software delivery lifecycle. In the subsequent sections of this chapter, we will delve deeper into the principles and practices that define DevOps and its significance in contemporary software engineering.

1.2 Defining DevOps: Principles and Practices

Defining DevOps goes beyond just describing it as a combination of development and operations. DevOps encompasses a set of principles and practices that guide the way software is developed, tested, and deployed. In this section, we will delve into the core concepts that define DevOps and explain how they shape the DevOps culture and methodology.

Key Principles of DevOps

1. Collaboration and Communication

At the heart of DevOps is the emphasis on collaboration and communication between development and operations teams. Traditionally, these teams operated in isolation, often leading to misunderstandings, finger-pointing, and delays. DevOps breaks down these silos, encouraging cross-functional teams that work together seamlessly. This collaboration results in a shared understanding of goals and responsibilities, leading to improved efficiency and quality.

2. Automation

Automation is a fundamental principle of DevOps. By automating repetitive tasks, such as code builds, testing, and deployment, DevOps aims to reduce human error, increase consistency, and accelerate the delivery process. Automation tools and scripts play a crucial role in achieving these goals, allowing teams to focus on higher-value tasks.

3. Continuous Integration (CI) and Continuous Deployment (CD)

Continuous Integration involves the practice of frequently integrating code changes into a shared repository and running automated tests. This ensures that code changes do not introduce defects and maintains code quality. Continuous Deployment takes CI a step further by automating the deployment of code changes to production as soon as they pass tests. These practices enable rapid and reliable software releases.

4. Infrastructure as Code (IaC)

IaC is a DevOps practice that treats infrastructure configuration as code. Instead of manually configuring servers and environments, infrastructure components are defined and managed using code. This approach provides version control, repeatability, and consistency in infrastructure provisioning, making it easier to manage complex and dynamic environments.

5. Monitoring and Feedback Loops

Effective monitoring and feedback loops are crucial for DevOps success. Real-time monitoring provides visibility into application performance, infrastructure health, and user experience. Feedback loops ensure that issues are detected early, allowing teams to respond quickly to incidents and continuously improve both the software and the processes.

DevOps Practices

DevOps principles are put into action through a set of practices that guide the development and deployment process:

- *Version Control*

Version control systems, such as Git, are essential for tracking changes in source code and configuration files. They enable collaboration, code history management, and the ability to revert to previous states if needed.

- *Automated Testing*

Automated testing is integral to DevOps, covering unit tests, integration tests, and end-to-end tests. These tests validate code changes, ensuring they meet quality standards and do not introduce regressions.

- *Containerization*

Containers, such as Docker, package applications and their dependencies into portable units. Containerization simplifies deployment, eliminates "it works on my machine" issues, and facilitates consistent environments.

- *Orchestration*

Orchestration tools, like Kubernetes, manage the deployment, scaling, and management of containerized applications. They provide automation for deploying and scaling services across clusters.

- Continuous Integration/Continuous Deployment (CI/CD) Pipelines

CI/CD pipelines automate the build, test, and deployment process. They integrate code changes, run tests, and deliver updates to production, ensuring a fast and reliable release cycle.

- Configuration Management

Configuration management tools, such as Ansible and Puppet, automate the configuration of servers and infrastructure. They ensure consistency and repeatability in server setups.

- Infrastructure as Code (IaC)

IaC tools, like Terraform, enable the definition and management of infrastructure using code. This practice ensures that infrastructure changes are versioned and can be reproduced reliably.

- Monitoring and Logging

Monitoring tools, such as Prometheus, collect metrics and alert on issues. Logging solutions, like ELK Stack, capture and analyze log data, providing insights into application and infrastructure performance.

In conclusion, DevOps is defined by its core principles of collaboration, automation, CI/CD, IaC, and monitoring, among others. These principles guide the adoption of specific practices that streamline software development, deployment, and operations. The result is a culture and methodology that enable organizations to deliver high-quality software rapidly and continuously adapt to changing requirements and customer needs.

1.3 The Importance of DevOps in Modern Software Engineering

DevOps has become a critical component of modern software engineering due to its ability to address the challenges and demands of today's software development landscape. In this section, we will explore why DevOps is essential in the context of contemporary software engineering.

Rapid Software Delivery

In the digital age, businesses are under constant pressure to deliver software faster to stay competitive. DevOps enables rapid software delivery through automation, continuous integration, and continuous deployment. By streamlining the development pipeline, DevOps allows organizations to release new features and updates more frequently, meeting the expectations of today's fast-paced market.

Enhanced Collaboration

Collaboration between development and operations teams is essential for efficient software delivery. DevOps promotes cross-functional collaboration, breaking down silos and fostering a culture of shared responsibility. This collaboration results in quicker problem-solving, improved communication, and a higher level of trust between teams.

Continuous Improvement

DevOps encourages a culture of continuous improvement. Teams regularly assess their processes, identify bottlenecks, and implement changes to enhance efficiency and quality. This iterative approach ensures that software development practices evolve to meet evolving business needs and customer expectations.

Reduced Risk

Traditional software development practices often involve manual interventions, leading to human errors and increased risk. DevOps mitigates these risks through automation, which eliminates many opportunities for mistakes. Additionally, automated testing and monitoring help detect issues early, reducing the likelihood of critical failures in production.

Cost Savings

DevOps can lead to cost savings through resource optimization and improved efficiency. By automating repetitive tasks, organizations can allocate resources more effectively, reducing the need for manual labor. Moreover, the faster delivery of features and bug fixes can result in increased revenue and customer satisfaction, ultimately contributing to cost savings.

Scalability

In a digital world, software needs to scale rapidly to accommodate user growth and changing demands. DevOps practices, such as containerization and orchestration, make it easier to scale applications and infrastructure. This scalability ensures that software can handle increased workloads without significant disruptions.

Improved Quality

Quality is a critical aspect of software development. DevOps emphasizes automated testing and continuous integration, which lead to higher code quality. By catching and addressing issues early in the development process, DevOps reduces the number of defects that make their way into production.

Customer-Centric Development

Modern software development is customer-centric, focusing on delivering features and improvements that align with customer needs. DevOps enables teams to gather real-time feedback from users and incorporate it into the development process. This feedback loop ensures that software remains relevant and valuable to customers.

Competitive Advantage

In today's competitive landscape, businesses that can deliver high-quality software quickly gain a significant advantage. DevOps allows organizations to respond to market changes swiftly, stay ahead of competitors, and innovate more effectively.

Regulatory Compliance

For industries with strict regulatory requirements, DevOps can assist in achieving and maintaining compliance. Automation and version control help ensure that code changes and infrastructure configurations adhere to compliance standards. This reduces the risk of non-compliance and associated penalties.

In summary, DevOps is of paramount importance in modern software engineering. It enables organizations to meet the challenges of rapid delivery, enhanced collaboration, continuous improvement, reduced risk, cost savings, scalability, improved quality, customer-centric development, competitive advantage, and regulatory compliance. As software continues to play a central role in business operations, DevOps remains a critical driver of success in the digital age.

1.4 Comparing Traditional IT and DevOps Approaches

In the world of software development and IT operations, two distinct approaches have emerged: the traditional IT approach and the DevOps approach. These approaches differ in their philosophies, practices, and outcomes. In this section, we will compare and contrast these two approaches to shed light on why DevOps has gained prominence.

Traditional IT Approach

The traditional IT approach to software development and operations follows a sequential and siloed model. It often involves the following characteristics:

- **Siloed Teams:** In traditional IT environments, development and operations teams operate independently and often have minimal communication. This leads to a lack of shared understanding and collaboration.

- **Manual Processes:** Many tasks, such as code deployment, configuration management, and testing, are performed manually. This manual intervention increases the likelihood of human errors and delays.

- **Long Release Cycles:** Traditional IT practices tend to have longer release cycles, with infrequent and substantial updates. This approach can result in slower responses to changing business requirements.

- **Limited Automation:** Automation is limited, and there is less emphasis on scripting and tools to streamline processes. As a result, repetitive tasks consume time and resources.

- **Risk of Failures:** With manual processes and limited automation, there is a higher risk of production failures and downtime. Identifying and addressing issues can be time-consuming.

- **Resistance to Change:** Traditional IT environments may resist change due to a fear of disrupting established processes. Change management can be complex and time-consuming.

DevOps Approach

DevOps, in contrast, represents a more modern and agile approach to software development and operations. It is characterized by the following:

- **Collaborative Teams:** DevOps promotes cross-functional collaboration, where development and operations teams work together as a single unit. This fosters better communication and shared accountability.

- **Automation:** Automation is a core principle of DevOps. Tasks like code integration, testing, deployment,

and infrastructure provisioning are automated to
minimize human intervention and reduce errors.

• **Continuous Integration/Continuous Deployment
(CI/CD):** DevOps emphasizes CI/CD pipelines,
allowing for the continuous integration of code changes,
automated testing, and rapid deployment to production.
This results in quicker and more reliable releases.

• **Infrastructure as Code (IaC):** DevOps leverages IaC
to manage infrastructure using code. This practice enables
version control, repeatability, and consistency in
infrastructure provisioning.

• **Monitoring and Feedback:** DevOps relies on real-time
monitoring and feedback loops to detect issues early and
drive continuous improvement. Teams are proactive in
identifying and addressing problems.

• **Embracing Change:** DevOps embraces change as a
natural part of the development process. It encourages
adaptability and responsiveness to evolving business
needs.

Contrasting Outcomes

The differences between traditional IT and DevOps approaches
manifest in the outcomes they produce:

• **Speed and Agility:** DevOps excels in speed and agility,
enabling organizations to release updates and features
quickly in response to market demands. Traditional IT
practices are often slower to adapt.

- **Quality and Reliability:** DevOps emphasizes automated testing and continuous integration, resulting in higher code quality and greater reliability. Traditional IT may experience more defects and production issues.

- **Cost Efficiency:** Automation and resource optimization in DevOps lead to cost efficiencies. Traditional IT may require more manual effort and resources, resulting in higher costs.

- **Customer Satisfaction:** DevOps's customer-centric approach, with rapid feature delivery and responsiveness to feedback, tends to enhance customer satisfaction. Traditional IT approaches may struggle to meet changing customer expectations.

- **Risk Mitigation:** DevOps's automation and monitoring help identify and mitigate risks early. Traditional IT practices may face higher risks of unplanned downtime and security vulnerabilities.

In summary, DevOps and traditional IT approaches represent two different paradigms in software development and operations. DevOps emphasizes collaboration, automation, continuous delivery, and adaptability, leading to faster, more reliable, and customer-centric outcomes. In contrast, traditional IT approaches tend to be more sequential, manual, and resistant to change, which can result in slower responses to business needs and a higher risk of issues. DevOps has gained prominence due to its ability to address the challenges of the modern software development landscape effectively.

1.5 Key Benefits of Adopting DevOps

The adoption of DevOps principles and practices offers a wide range of benefits to organizations across various industries. In this section, we will explore some of the key advantages that come with embracing DevOps in the context of software development and IT operations.

1. Improved Collaboration

One of the primary benefits of adopting DevOps is the enhancement of collaboration between development and operations teams. By breaking down silos and fostering a culture of shared responsibility, DevOps encourages teams to work together seamlessly. This collaboration leads to better communication, alignment of goals, and a deeper understanding of each other's roles and challenges.

2. Faster Time-to-Market

DevOps practices, such as automation, continuous integration, and continuous deployment, enable organizations to accelerate the delivery of software and updates. With shorter development cycles and automated testing, code changes can move swiftly from development to production. This speed-to-market advantage allows businesses to respond rapidly to market demands and gain a competitive edge.

3. Increased Reliability

Automation in DevOps reduces the risk of human errors, leading to greater reliability in software delivery. Continuous integration ensures that code changes are thoroughly tested, and automated deployment pipelines guarantee consistent and error-free releases.

As a result, organizations can deliver high-quality software with fewer defects and production failures.

4. Enhanced Quality

Quality is a paramount focus in DevOps. Automated testing and continuous monitoring help maintain and improve code quality throughout the development process. By catching and addressing issues early, DevOps teams ensure that the software meets or exceeds quality standards, resulting in a better user experience.

5. Cost Efficiency

DevOps practices promote resource optimization and efficiency. Automation reduces the need for manual labor, leading to cost savings in terms of both time and human resources. Organizations can allocate their resources more effectively, optimizing their budgets and investments.

6. Agility and Adaptability

DevOps embraces change as a natural part of the software development process. The ability to adapt quickly to changing business requirements and customer feedback is a significant advantage. DevOps teams can pivot, iterate, and innovate more effectively to meet evolving needs.

7. Continuous Feedback and Improvement

DevOps emphasizes the importance of continuous feedback loops. Real-time monitoring and feedback mechanisms provide insights into application performance and user experience. This feedback drives ongoing improvement, helping organizations make data-driven decisions and refine their processes.

8. Scalability

In a digital world where scalability is crucial, DevOps practices make it easier to scale applications and infrastructure. Containerization and orchestration tools enable organizations to handle increased workloads and growth without significant disruptions or delays.

9. Competitive Advantage

DevOps enables organizations to respond rapidly to market changes and customer demands. The ability to release new features and updates quickly gives businesses a competitive advantage, allowing them to innovate and stay ahead of competitors.

10. Risk Mitigation

Through automation, monitoring, and early issue detection, DevOps helps mitigate risks in software development and operations. By identifying and addressing issues proactively, organizations reduce the likelihood of unplanned downtime and security vulnerabilities.

In summary, adopting DevOps practices offers a multitude of benefits, including improved collaboration, faster time-to-market, increased reliability, enhanced quality, cost efficiency, agility, continuous feedback and improvement, scalability, competitive advantage, and risk mitigation. These advantages make DevOps a compelling approach for organizations seeking to streamline their software delivery processes and achieve better outcomes in a rapidly evolving digital landscape.

Chapter 2: DevOps Culture and Mindset

2.1 Building a DevOps Culture: Collaboration and Communication

Building a DevOps culture is foundational to the successful implementation of DevOps principles and practices. A DevOps culture is characterized by collaboration, communication, and a shared mindset among teams involved in software development and operations. In this section, we will explore the key components of building a DevOps culture that fosters collaboration and effective communication.

Collaboration Across Silos

In traditional IT environments, development and operations teams often operate in separate silos with limited interaction. In contrast, DevOps promotes the breaking down of these silos to create cross-functional teams where developers, operations personnel, and other stakeholders collaborate seamlessly. This collaborative approach eliminates the "us versus them" mentality and encourages a sense of shared ownership and responsibility for the entire software delivery process.

Communication and Transparency

Effective communication is at the core of a DevOps culture. Teams need to communicate openly, transparently, and frequently. This includes sharing project updates, progress reports, and feedback. DevOps encourages the use of collaboration tools, chat platforms, and shared documentation to facilitate communication, ensuring that everyone is on the same page.

Cross-Training and Skill Sharing

In a DevOps culture, team members are encouraged to broaden their skills and knowledge beyond their core roles. Cross-training allows developers to understand the operational challenges and constraints, while operations personnel gain insights into the development process. This cross-pollination of skills leads to better problem-solving, empathy between teams, and a deeper understanding of the entire software lifecycle.

Empowering Teams

Empowered teams have the autonomy to make decisions and take ownership of their work. DevOps promotes a culture where teams are given the authority and responsibility to make choices about the tools, processes, and technologies they use. Empowerment fosters creativity, innovation, and a sense of ownership, which are essential for driving continuous improvement.

Embracing Failure as a Learning Opportunity

A DevOps culture views failures as opportunities for learning and growth rather than as reasons for blame. When something goes wrong, teams conduct post-mortems to analyze the root causes and identify preventive measures. This approach encourages a blame-free environment where individuals are not afraid to experiment and take calculated risks.

Aligning Goals and Metrics

To promote collaboration, it's essential to align the goals and metrics of development and operations teams. This alignment ensures that everyone is working towards the same objectives. Common metrics, such as deployment frequency, lead time, and error rates, help teams track progress and measure the impact of their efforts.

Leadership Support

Building a DevOps culture requires strong leadership support. Leaders set the tone for collaboration, communication, and cultural change within an organization. They must actively endorse and promote DevOps principles, provide resources, and foster an environment where experimentation and innovation are encouraged.

Continuous Feedback and Improvement

DevOps culture encourages continuous feedback and improvement. Teams regularly gather feedback from users, stakeholders, and each other. This feedback loop allows for the identification of areas that need enhancement and drives the iterative improvement of processes and practices.

Case Studies: Successful DevOps Culture Implementations

Throughout this chapter, we will explore case studies of organizations that have successfully transformed their culture to embrace DevOps principles. These real-world examples provide valuable insights into the challenges faced, the strategies employed, and the outcomes achieved in building a DevOps culture that promotes collaboration, communication, and a mindset of continuous improvement.

In summary, building a DevOps culture is fundamental to the success of DevOps initiatives. It involves breaking down silos, fostering collaboration, promoting open communication, encouraging cross-training, empowering teams, embracing failure as a learning opportunity, aligning goals and metrics, gaining leadership support, and establishing a culture of continuous feedback and improvement. A DevOps culture sets the stage for the effective implementation of DevOps practices and the achievement of its key benefits.

2.2 Overcoming Resistance to Change

In the journey to establish a DevOps culture and mindset, one of the significant challenges organizations often encounter is resistance to change. Resistance can come from various sources within an organization, including team members, managers, and stakeholders. In this section, we will explore the common reasons for resistance to DevOps and strategies to overcome it.

Reasons for Resistance

1. Fear of the Unknown

Change can be intimidating, especially when it involves adopting new practices and technologies. Team members may fear the unknown and worry about their ability to adapt to DevOps principles and practices. They might be comfortable with existing processes and reluctant to embrace something unfamiliar.

2. Cultural Inertia

Organizations often have established cultures and ways of working that have been in place for years. DevOps represents a significant cultural shift, and some individuals may resist changing long-standing practices and norms.

3. Lack of Understanding

Resistance can stem from a lack of understanding of DevOps concepts and benefits. Team members may not fully grasp how DevOps can improve their daily work or the overall success of the organization. This lack of understanding can lead to skepticism.

4. Fear of Job Insecurity

There may be concerns about job security when automation is introduced. Team members might worry that automated processes will replace their roles. It's crucial to communicate that automation frees up time for more value-added tasks rather than eliminating jobs.

5. Silo Mentality

In organizations with a strong silo mentality, different teams may resist DevOps because it challenges their established roles and responsibilities. Breaking down these silos can be met with resistance from those who feel threatened by changes to their domain.

Strategies to Overcome Resistance

1. Education and Training

One of the most effective ways to overcome resistance is through education and training. Providing team members with resources, workshops, and training programs that explain DevOps concepts and benefits can help demystify the process and alleviate fears.

2. Effective Communication

Open and transparent communication is critical. Leaders and advocates for DevOps should regularly communicate the vision, goals, and benefits of DevOps adoption. Addressing concerns and providing regular updates can help build trust and reduce resistance.

3. Pilot Projects

Initiating small-scale pilot projects can be a powerful strategy. Starting with a limited scope allows teams to gain experience with DevOps practices in a controlled environment. Success in these pilot projects can serve as proof of concept and encourage wider adoption.

4. Cross-Functional Collaboration

Encourage cross-functional collaboration by creating DevOps teams that include members from both development and operations. Collaborative teams can demonstrate the benefits of breaking down silos and working together effectively.

5. Leadership Support

Strong leadership support is essential in overcoming resistance. Leaders should champion the DevOps transformation, set an example by embracing the culture themselves, and provide the necessary resources and incentives to motivate teams.

6. Feedback and Adaptation

Collect feedback from team members throughout the adoption process and be willing to adapt. Address concerns, modify processes, and make improvements based on feedback. This demonstrates that the organization values input and is committed to continuous improvement.

7. Celebrate Successes

Recognize and celebrate achievements along the DevOps journey. Whether it's a successful deployment, reduced lead time, or improved collaboration, acknowledging these wins reinforces the positive aspects of DevOps.

8. Change Management

Implement effective change management practices. This includes assessing the impact of DevOps on different roles, addressing concerns, and creating a roadmap for change that involves all stakeholders.

9. Metrics and Progress Tracking

Establish metrics to track progress and demonstrate the benefits of DevOps. Metrics related to deployment frequency, lead time, error rates, and customer satisfaction can help showcase improvements.

10. Patience and Persistence

Overcoming resistance to change is not always quick or straightforward. It requires patience and persistence. Continue to iterate and refine strategies as necessary to make steady progress.

In summary, overcoming resistance to DevOps adoption is crucial for building a DevOps culture and mindset. Resistance can arise from fear of the unknown, cultural inertia, lack of understanding, job security concerns, and the silo mentality. To address resistance effectively, organizations should employ strategies such as education and training, effective communication, pilot projects, cross-functional collaboration, leadership support, feedback mechanisms, celebration of successes, change management, metrics tracking, and a patient and persistent approach. By addressing resistance head-on, organizations can pave the way for successful DevOps transformation and reap the benefits it offers.

2.3 The Role of Leadership in DevOps Transformation

Effective leadership plays a pivotal role in driving and sustaining a successful DevOps transformation within an organization. Leaders at all levels, from executives to middle management, have a significant impact on the cultural shift and adoption of DevOps principles and practices. In this section, we will explore the key roles and responsibilities of leadership in a DevOps transformation.

Setting the Vision

Leadership's first and foremost responsibility in a DevOps transformation is to set a clear and compelling vision. This vision should outline the organization's goals, the desired DevOps culture, and the expected benefits. By articulating the vision, leaders inspire teams and create a shared sense of purpose.

Advocating for Change

Leaders need to be vocal advocates for DevOps principles and practices. They should communicate the importance of the transformation, its alignment with business objectives, and the value it brings. Advocacy from leadership helps overcome resistance and encourages buy-in from team members at all levels.

Providing Resources and Support

To enable a DevOps transformation, leaders must allocate the necessary resources, including budget, tools, training, and skilled personnel. They should provide the support required to implement DevOps practices effectively. This support may involve investing in automation tools, training programs, and infrastructure improvements.

Leading by Example

Leaders should lead by example and demonstrate their commitment to DevOps. This means actively participating in the cultural shift, embracing new practices, and continuously learning. When leaders champion DevOps, it sends a powerful message to the organization.

Removing Barriers

Leaders must identify and eliminate barriers that hinder the DevOps transformation. This includes addressing organizational silos, streamlining processes, and breaking down communication barriers. Leaders should be proactive in removing obstacles that impede progress.

Empowering Teams

Empowerment is a crucial aspect of leadership in DevOps. Leaders should empower teams to make decisions, take ownership, and experiment. Teams need the autonomy to choose the tools and practices that work best for them within the DevOps framework.

Creating a Learning Culture

Leaders should promote a culture of continuous learning and improvement. They should encourage teams to seek out opportunities for skill development, experimentation, and knowledge sharing. A learning culture fosters innovation and adaptation.

Aligning Metrics with Objectives

Leaders should ensure that metrics and key performance indicators (KPIs) align with the DevOps transformation objectives. Metrics related to deployment frequency, lead time, error rates, and customer satisfaction should be tracked and used to measure progress and success.

Providing Regular Feedback

Feedback is essential in any transformation. Leaders should provide constructive feedback to teams and individuals, acknowledging their efforts and helping them identify areas for improvement. Regular feedback fosters growth and development.

Supporting Risk-Taking

In a DevOps environment, risk-taking is encouraged as long as it is calculated and well-managed. Leaders should create an environment where individuals feel safe to take risks, experiment, and learn from failures. Innovation often arises from taking calculated risks.

Measuring and Celebrating Success

Leaders should actively measure and celebrate the successes achieved through the DevOps transformation. Celebrations can take the form of recognition, rewards, or simply acknowledging milestones. Celebrating successes reinforces the positive aspects of DevOps and motivates teams.

Sustaining the Transformation

A DevOps transformation is an ongoing journey. Leaders should ensure that the transformation is sustained over time by regularly revisiting the vision, reassessing goals, and adapting to changing circumstances. Continuous improvement is at the heart of DevOps.

Case Studies: Leadership in DevOps

Throughout this chapter, we will examine case studies of organizations where effective leadership played a crucial role in the successful implementation of DevOps practices. These real-world examples provide insights into how leadership can drive cultural change and deliver tangible benefits.

In summary, leadership plays a pivotal role in a DevOps transformation. Leaders set the vision, advocate for change, provide resources, lead by example, remove barriers, empower teams, create a learning culture, align metrics, provide feedback, support risk-taking, measure and celebrate success, and sustain the transformation. Effective leadership is instrumental in fostering a DevOps culture and realizing the benefits of DevOps within an organization.

2.4 Fostering Continuous Learning and Improvement

Continuous learning and improvement are fundamental aspects of a DevOps culture and mindset. In this section, we will delve into the importance of fostering a culture of continuous learning and improvement within DevOps teams and organizations.

The Learning Organization

A learning organization is one that values and promotes continuous learning and improvement at all levels. In a DevOps context, this means encouraging individuals and teams to acquire new skills, adapt to change, and embrace innovation. Learning organizations prioritize knowledge sharing and actively seek ways to enhance their processes.

Continuous Learning

DevOps promotes the concept of continuous learning, where individuals are encouraged to acquire new knowledge and skills continuously. This learning can take various forms, including:

1. Training and Certification

Providing training opportunities and certifications in DevOps practices and tools is a common way to facilitate continuous learning. Team members can enhance their expertise and stay up-to-date with industry best practices.

2. Communities of Practice

Creating communities of practice within an organization allows like-minded individuals to come together to share knowledge and experiences. These communities can focus on specific aspects of DevOps, such as automation, continuous integration, or containerization.

3. Cross-Functional Training

Cross-training team members in different roles (e.g., developers learning about operations, and vice versa) enhances collaboration and understanding. This enables teams to work more cohesively and address challenges collectively.

4. Conferences and Events

Attending DevOps conferences, webinars, and industry events provides opportunities to learn from experts, hear about emerging trends, and network with peers. These events can inspire new ideas and approaches.

5. Online Resources

The internet offers a wealth of online resources, including blogs, forums, documentation, and tutorials. Team members can leverage these resources to stay informed and expand their knowledge.

A Culture of Experimentation

In a DevOps culture, experimentation is encouraged. Team members are empowered to try new tools, practices, and approaches. Experimentation provides opportunities to discover innovative solutions, identify best practices, and learn from failures. It fosters a culture of continuous improvement.

Feedback Loops

Feedback loops are a critical component of continuous learning and improvement. DevOps teams establish feedback mechanisms that allow them to gather insights from various sources, including users, stakeholders, and performance monitoring. Feedback helps teams identify areas for enhancement and refine their processes.

Kaizen and Continuous Improvement

The concept of Kaizen, which originated in Japanese manufacturing, emphasizes continuous improvement. In DevOps, teams embrace this philosophy by regularly assessing their processes and looking for ways to make incremental enhancements. Continuous improvement is not about making drastic changes but rather about making small, consistent improvements over time.

Agile Practices

DevOps is closely aligned with Agile principles, which emphasize adaptability and responsiveness to change. Agile practices, such as sprint retrospectives in Scrum, provide opportunities for teams to reflect on their work, identify areas for improvement, and plan for adjustments in the next iteration.

Tools for Continuous Improvement

Various tools and practices support continuous improvement in DevOps:

- **Automated Testing:** Automated testing ensures that code changes are thoroughly tested, helping identify defects early and reducing the risk of issues in production.

- **Monitoring and Alerting:** Real-time monitoring and alerting systems provide insights into application performance and facilitate rapid responses to issues.

- **Metrics and Key Performance Indicators (KPIs):** Tracking metrics related to deployment frequency, lead time, error rates, and customer satisfaction helps measure progress and identify areas for improvement.

- **Post-Mortems and Incident Analysis:** Conducting post-mortems and incident analyses following production incidents provides valuable lessons and opportunities for process improvement.

Case Studies: Continuous Learning and Improvement

Throughout this chapter, we will explore case studies of organizations that have successfully fostered a culture of continuous learning and improvement in their DevOps initiatives. These case studies highlight the benefits of embracing a culture of learning and how it contributes to achieving DevOps goals.

In conclusion, fostering continuous learning and improvement is a core element of a DevOps culture and mindset. Organizations that prioritize learning and encourage experimentation, feedback loops, and Kaizen are better equipped to adapt to change, innovate, and continually enhance their processes. Continuous learning and improvement are essential for realizing the full potential of DevOps and delivering high-quality software efficiently.

2.5 Case Studies: Successful DevOps Culture Implementations

In this section, we will examine real-world case studies of organizations that have successfully implemented a DevOps culture. These case studies offer insights into the challenges these organizations faced, the strategies they employed, and the outcomes they achieved in building a DevOps culture that promotes collaboration, communication, and continuous improvement.

Case Study 1: Amazon Web Services (AWS)

Amazon Web Services (AWS) is one of the leading cloud computing platforms globally and a prominent example of a successful DevOps culture implementation. AWS embraced DevOps principles to enhance its cloud services and infrastructure operations. Key takeaways from AWS's DevOps journey include:

- **Automation at Scale:** AWS automated its infrastructure provisioning, enabling rapid scalability. The company uses tools like AWS CloudFormation to define and provision resources through code.

- **Continuous Deployment:** AWS practices continuous deployment, allowing for frequent updates and improvements to its services. This approach ensures that customers always have access to the latest features and enhancements.

- **Customer-Centric Approach:** AWS's DevOps culture is driven by a focus on customer needs. This customer-centric approach ensures that AWS continuously listens to customer feedback and adapts its services accordingly.

- **Culture of Experimentation:** AWS encourages a culture of experimentation, allowing teams to innovate and test new ideas. This approach has led to the development of new services and features.

Case Study 2: Etsy

Etsy, an e-commerce platform for handmade and vintage items, is renowned for its successful DevOps adoption. Key aspects of Etsy's DevOps culture implementation include:

- **Blameless Post-Mortems:** Etsy emphasizes blameless post-mortems, where incidents are reviewed to learn from mistakes rather than assigning blame. This approach fosters a culture of transparency and continuous improvement.

- **Collaborative Culture:** Etsy encourages cross-functional collaboration between development and operations teams. Engineers are responsible for deploying their code, promoting shared ownership and accountability.

- **ChatOps:** Etsy uses ChatOps, a practice that integrates chat tools with automation, to facilitate communication and collaboration. ChatOps allows engineers to perform tasks and receive notifications within chat platforms, streamlining operations.

- **Data-Driven Decisions:** Etsy relies on data to drive decision-making. Metrics and monitoring play a crucial role in identifying issues, measuring performance, and making informed choices for improvements.

Case Study 3: Netflix

Netflix, a global streaming platform, is a pioneer in implementing DevOps practices to support its massive infrastructure and continuous delivery of content. Key elements of Netflix's DevOps culture include:

- **Chaos Engineering:** Netflix is known for its Chaos Engineering practice, where engineers deliberately introduce failures into their systems to test resilience. This approach helps Netflix identify vulnerabilities and build more robust systems.

- **Microservices Architecture:** Netflix adopted a microservices architecture, breaking down its application into small, independently deployable services. This approach enhances agility and accelerates development.

- **Automated Testing:** Netflix relies heavily on automated testing, ensuring that changes do not introduce regressions. Automated testing contributes to the platform's high reliability.

- **Open Source Contributions:** Netflix actively contributes to open source projects and shares its DevOps tools and practices with the community. This demonstrates a commitment to collaborative improvement.

Case Study 4: Target

Target, a major retail corporation, embraced DevOps to enhance its software development and operations. Key aspects of Target's DevOps culture implementation include:

- **DevOps Academy:** Target established a DevOps Academy to train its employees and ensure that they have the necessary skills to embrace DevOps practices.

- **Cross-Functional Teams:** Target reorganized its teams to be cross-functional, with members from various disciplines working closely together. This approach promotes collaboration and shared responsibility.

- **Automated Testing and Deployment:** Target implemented automated testing and deployment pipelines to accelerate software delivery while maintaining quality.

- **Feedback-Driven Development:** Target prioritizes customer feedback and uses it to drive product improvements. This customer-centric approach aligns with DevOps principles.

These case studies highlight the diversity of organizations that have successfully implemented DevOps cultures, demonstrating that DevOps is not limited to a specific industry or company size. The common threads among these success stories include a commitment to automation, collaboration, continuous learning, customer-centricity, and a culture that embraces experimentation and learning from failures.

Chapter 3: Tools and Technologies for DevOps

3.1 Overview of Essential DevOps Tools

In this section, we will provide an overview of essential DevOps tools commonly used by organizations to support and streamline their DevOps practices. These tools play a crucial role in automating processes, facilitating collaboration, and ensuring the smooth delivery of software. It's important to note that the DevOps toolchain may vary based on specific requirements and technologies used by each organization.

Version Control Systems

Git

Git is a distributed version control system that allows teams to track changes to their source code, collaborate on code development, and manage multiple versions of a project. Git is highly popular and is the foundation for many DevOps workflows.

Continuous Integration and Continuous Deployment (CI/CD) Tools

Jenkins

Jenkins is an open-source automation server used for building, testing, and deploying code. It provides a wide range of plugins that enable integration with various tools and platforms, making it a versatile choice for CI/CD pipelines.

Travis CI

Travis CI is a cloud-based CI/CD service that automates the build and testing process. It integrates seamlessly with popular version control systems like GitHub and supports a wide range of programming languages.

CircleCI

CircleCI is another cloud-based CI/CD platform that automates the software delivery process. It offers a scalable and flexible solution for building and deploying applications.

Infrastructure as Code (IaC) Tools

Terraform

Terraform is an open-source IaC tool that allows infrastructure to be defined as code. It supports various cloud providers and enables the provisioning and management of infrastructure resources using code.

Ansible

Ansible is an open-source automation tool that facilitates configuration management, application deployment, and task automation. It uses a simple and human-readable YAML syntax for defining automation tasks.

Containerization and Orchestration

Docker

Docker is a popular containerization platform that allows applications and their dependencies to be packaged into containers. Containers provide consistency and portability across different environments.

Kubernetes

Kubernetes is an open-source container orchestration platform for automating the deployment, scaling, and management of containerized applications. It provides features for container orchestration, load balancing, and automated scaling.

Monitoring and Logging Tools

Prometheus

Prometheus is an open-source monitoring and alerting toolkit designed for reliability and scalability. It collects and stores metrics from various systems and applications, making it a valuable tool for observability.

ELK Stack (Elasticsearch, Logstash, Kibana)

The ELK Stack is a set of tools used for log management and analysis. Elasticsearch stores and indexes logs, Logstash processes and filters log data, and Kibana provides a visualization and dashboarding interface for log analysis.

Collaboration and Communication Tools

Slack

Slack is a popular team collaboration platform that facilitates communication and collaboration among DevOps teams. It offers channels for real-time messaging, file sharing, and integration with other DevOps tools.

Microsoft Teams

Microsoft Teams is another team collaboration platform that provides chat, video conferencing, and file sharing features. It integrates seamlessly with Microsoft 365 and offers a range of third-party integrations.

Configuration Management Tools

Puppet

Puppet is a configuration management tool that automates the provisioning and management of infrastructure. It uses a declarative language to define system configurations and enforce them across servers.

Chef

Chef is another configuration management tool that allows for infrastructure automation and application deployment. It uses recipes to define configurations and ensure consistency.

Security and Compliance Tools

SonarQube

SonarQube is an open-source platform for continuous inspection of code quality and security. It identifies code issues, vulnerabilities, and maintains code quality standards.

OWASP ZAP

OWASP Zed Attack Proxy (ZAP) is a security testing tool used to find security vulnerabilities in web applications during development and testing phases. It helps identify and remediate security issues.

Testing and Quality Assurance Tools

Selenium

Selenium is an open-source testing framework for automating web browsers. It allows for automated testing of web applications across different browsers and platforms.

JUnit

JUnit is a widely used testing framework for Java applications. It provides annotations and assertions to write and execute unit tests for Java code.

Collaboration and Integration Platforms

GitHub

GitHub is a web-based platform for version control and collaboration. It provides features for code hosting, pull requests, issue tracking, and integrations with CI/CD tools.

GitLab

GitLab is a web-based platform similar to GitHub but offers an integrated DevOps platform that includes CI/CD pipelines, container registry, and collaboration features.

Conclusion

These are some of the essential DevOps tools and technologies that organizations commonly use to support their DevOps practices. The selection of tools may vary depending on specific project requirements, technology stack, and organizational preferences. An effective DevOps toolchain streamlines processes, improves collaboration, and accelerates the delivery of high-quality software.

3.2 Continuous Integration and Continuous Deployment (CI/CD)

Continuous Integration (CI) and Continuous Deployment (CD) are integral components of DevOps practices, enabling teams to automate the building, testing, and deployment of software. In this section, we will explore CI/CD principles, benefits, and commonly used tools.

Principles of CI/CD

1. Automation

Automation is at the core of CI/CD. It involves automating tasks such as code compilation, testing, and deployment. Automation ensures consistency and reduces the likelihood of human errors.

2. Version Control

Version control systems like Git play a pivotal role in CI/CD. Developers commit their code changes to a shared repository, allowing for collaboration and tracking of changes over time.

3. Continuous Integration

Continuous Integration is the practice of frequently integrating code changes into a shared repository. This process triggers automated builds and tests to detect issues early. CI encourages smaller, more frequent code changes.

4. Automated Testing

Automated testing is crucial for ensuring the reliability and quality of code. It includes unit tests, integration tests, and end-to-end tests. Automated tests are executed as part of the CI/CD pipeline.

5. Continuous Deployment

Continuous Deployment automates the release process, allowing tested code changes to be deployed to production automatically. It aims to reduce manual intervention in the deployment process.

Benefits of CI/CD

1. Faster Release Cycles

CI/CD pipelines enable rapid and frequent releases, allowing organizations to respond quickly to customer needs and market changes.

2. Improved Code Quality

Automated testing and code validation in CI/CD pipelines help catch bugs and issues early in the development process, leading to higher code quality.

3. Reduced Risk

Automated deployments reduce the risk associated with manual deployments, as they are less prone to human error.

4. Collaboration

CI/CD encourages collaboration among development, testing, and operations teams. It promotes a shared understanding of the software delivery process.

5. Efficiency

CI/CD automates repetitive tasks, saving time and effort for development and operations teams. This efficiency allows teams to focus on innovation and improvements.

CI/CD Tools

Jenkins

Jenkins is a widely used open-source CI/CD tool that provides a range of plugins and integrations. It supports building, testing, and deploying code across various platforms and environments.

Travis CI

Travis CI is a cloud-based CI/CD service that integrates seamlessly with popular version control systems like GitHub. It offers ease of use and is suitable for smaller projects.

CircleCI

CircleCI is a cloud-based CI/CD platform known for its scalability and flexibility. It allows teams to build, test, and deploy code efficiently.

GitLab CI/CD

GitLab CI/CD is tightly integrated with GitLab and provides a complete DevOps platform. It offers a built-in CI/CD pipeline configuration and management.

GitHub Actions

GitHub Actions is GitHub's native CI/CD solution. It enables developers to automate workflows directly within their GitHub repositories.

Travis CI

Travis CI is a cloud-based CI/CD service that integrates seamlessly with popular version control systems like GitHub. It offers ease of use and is suitable for smaller projects.

CI/CD Pipeline

A typical CI/CD pipeline consists of the following stages:

1. **Code Commit:** Developers commit their code changes to a version control system like Git.
2. **Build:** The CI/CD pipeline automatically builds the code, compiling it into executable artifacts.
3. **Automated Testing:** Automated tests, including unit tests, integration tests, and other validations, are executed.
4. **Artifact Generation:** If all tests pass, the pipeline generates deployable artifacts.
5. **Deployment:** In the CD phase, the pipeline deploys the artifacts to a staging or production environment.
6. **Monitoring and Feedback:** Continuous monitoring and feedback mechanisms track the application's performance and collect user feedback.
7. **Rollback (if necessary):** In case of issues, automated rollback mechanisms can revert the deployment to a stable state.

CI/CD Best Practices

- **Start Simple:** Begin with a basic CI/CD pipeline and gradually expand its complexity as needed.

- **Automate Everything:** Automate as many tasks as possible, including testing, deployment, and rollback.

- **Monitor and Measure:** Implement monitoring to gain insights into pipeline performance and application behavior.

- **Security:** Include security testing and vulnerability scanning in your pipeline.

- **Documentation:** Document the CI/CD pipeline and its processes to ensure clarity and understanding.

In summary, CI/CD is a fundamental practice in DevOps that emphasizes automation, collaboration, and continuous improvement. It accelerates software delivery, improves code quality, reduces risk, and enhances efficiency. A variety of CI/CD tools are available, each with its own strengths, allowing organizations to choose the best fit for their needs.

3.3 Infrastructure as Code (IaC)

Infrastructure as Code (IaC) is a fundamental practice in DevOps that involves managing and provisioning infrastructure resources through code. It enables teams to automate the setup and configuration of infrastructure, improving efficiency, consistency, and scalability. In this section, we will explore the principles of IaC, its benefits, and commonly used IaC tools.

Principles of IaC

1. Declarative Configuration

IaC follows a declarative approach, where the desired state of the infrastructure is defined in code. Instead of specifying step-by-step instructions, you declare what the infrastructure should look like, and the IaC tool ensures that state is achieved.

2. Version Control

IaC code is typically stored in version control systems like Git, allowing teams to track changes, collaborate, and roll back to previous configurations if needed.

3. Automation

IaC automates the provisioning and management of infrastructure, reducing manual intervention and the risk of human errors. This automation accelerates infrastructure deployment.

4. Consistency

IaC ensures that infrastructure remains consistent across different environments, such as development, testing, staging, and production. This consistency reduces the "works on my machine" problem.

5. Scalability

IaC enables the dynamic scaling of infrastructure resources to meet changing demands. Scaling can be accomplished by adjusting code configurations.

Benefits of IaC

1. Speed and Agility

IaC accelerates infrastructure provisioning, allowing teams to respond quickly to changing requirements and scale resources as needed.

2. Consistency

IaC ensures that infrastructure configurations are consistent across environments, reducing deployment and operational issues.

3. Version Control

Infrastructure code can be versioned, providing a history of changes and enabling collaboration among team members.

4. Cost Efficiency

Automated infrastructure provisioning reduces manual labor, leading to cost savings and efficient resource utilization.

5. Disaster Recovery

With IaC, recreating infrastructure in the event of a disaster is faster and more reliable since the entire configuration is defined in code.

IaC Tools

Terraform

Terraform is an open-source IaC tool developed by HashiCorp. It uses a declarative configuration language and supports various cloud providers, virtualization platforms, and on-premises infrastructure.

Example Terraform Configuration for AWS:

```
# Define an AWS EC2 instance

resource "aws_instance" "example" {

ami = "ami-0c55b159cbfafe1f0"

instance_type = "t2.micro"

}

# Define a security group

resource "aws_security_group" "example" {

name_prefix = "example-"

}

# Allow incoming HTTP traffic

ingress {

from_port = 80

to_port = 80

protocol = "tcp"
```

```
cidr_blocks = ["0.0.0.0/0"]

}

# Associate the security group with the EC2 instance

resource "aws_instance" "example" {

security_groups = [aws_security_group.example.name]

}
```

Ansible

Ansible is an open-source automation tool that can be used for infrastructure provisioning, configuration management, and application deployment. It uses a human-readable YAML syntax for defining tasks.

Example Ansible Playbook for Installing Nginx:

—-

```
- name: Install Nginx

hosts: web_servers

tasks:

- name: Update apt package cache

apt:

update_cache: yes

- name: Install Nginx

apt:
```

```
name: nginx

state: present

- name: Start Nginx service

service:

name: nginx

state: started

enabled: yes
```

AWS CloudFormation

AWS CloudFormation is a service provided by Amazon Web Services for defining and provisioning AWS infrastructure as code. It uses JSON or YAML templates to describe AWS resources and their configurations.

Example AWS CloudFormation Template for an EC2 Instance:

```
Resources:

MyEC2Instance:

Type: AWS::EC2::Instance

Properties:

ImageId: ami-0c55b159cbfafe1f0

InstanceType: t2.micro
```

Kubernetes Manifests

In the context of container orchestration, Kubernetes manifests (YAML files) are often used to define and manage the desired state of Kubernetes resources such as pods, services, and deployments.

Example Kubernetes Deployment Manifest:

```
apiVersion: apps/v1

kind: Deployment

metadata:

name: my-app

spec:

replicas: 3

selector:

matchLabels:

app: my-app

template:

metadata:

labels:

app: my-app

spec:

containers:

- name: my-app-container
```

image: my-app:latest

IaC Best Practices

- **Modularity:** Break down infrastructure code into reusable modules for better maintain

---

3.4 Monitoring and Logging in a DevOps Environment

Monitoring and logging are essential components of a DevOps environment, providing visibility into system performance, detecting issues, and facilitating troubleshooting. In this section, we will explore the importance of monitoring and logging, key practices, and commonly used tools in DevOps.

Importance of Monitoring and Logging

1. Performance Visibility

Monitoring tools provide real-time insights into the performance of applications and infrastructure, helping teams identify bottlenecks, slow response times, and resource utilization.

2. Issue Detection

Monitoring allows the early detection of issues, such as system failures, application errors, or performance degradation. This proactive approach helps teams address problems before they impact users.

3. Troubleshooting

Logs serve as a valuable resource for troubleshooting issues. They contain detailed information about events, errors, and system behavior, aiding in the root cause analysis.

4. Performance Optimization

Monitoring data helps optimize system performance by identifying areas for improvement. Teams can use metrics to make informed decisions about resource allocation and scalability.

5. Compliance and Security

Monitoring and logging are critical for compliance with security standards and regulations. They provide audit trails and evidence of security-related events.

Monitoring Practices

1. Define Key Metrics

Identify key performance indicators (KPIs) and metrics that align with your application's goals and user experience. Examples include response time, error rate, and resource utilization.

2. Set Thresholds

Establish thresholds for metrics to trigger alerts when values exceed acceptable limits. Thresholds help identify abnormal behavior.

3. Real-Time Monitoring

Implement real-time monitoring to receive immediate alerts and responses to critical events. This allows for rapid incident resolution.

4. Historical Data

Store historical monitoring data to track trends over time, aiding in capacity planning and long-term performance optimization.

Logging Practices

1. Centralized Logging

Aggregate logs from different sources, such as application servers, databases, and infrastructure components, into a centralized logging system for easy access and analysis.

2. Structured Logging

Use structured log formats, such as JSON or key-value pairs, to facilitate log parsing and analysis. Structured logs make it easier to extract meaningful information.

3. Log Rotation

Implement log rotation to manage log file sizes and prevent them from consuming excessive storage space. Log rotation ensures that older logs are archived or deleted.

4. Log Retention Policies

Define log retention policies to determine how long logs should be retained. Compliance requirements and operational needs influence these policies.

Monitoring and Logging Tools

Prometheus

Prometheus is an open-source monitoring and alerting toolkit designed for reliability and scalability. It collects metrics from various systems and applications, making it suitable for observability.

Grafana

Grafana is an open-source platform for creating and sharing interactive dashboards and visualizations. It can be integrated with Prometheus for real-time monitoring.

ELK Stack (Elasticsearch, Logstash, Kibana)

The ELK Stack is a set of tools used for log management and analysis. Elasticsearch stores and indexes logs, Logstash processes and filters log data, and Kibana provides a visualization and dashboarding interface for log analysis.

Splunk

Splunk is a comprehensive platform for log management, analytics, and visualization. It offers real-time monitoring, alerts, and advanced search capabilities.

New Relic

New Relic provides application performance monitoring (APM) and infrastructure monitoring. It offers insights into application performance and user experience.

Datadog

Datadog is a cloud-based monitoring and analytics platform that provides real-time visibility into infrastructure, applications, and logs.

Implementing Monitoring and Logging

To implement monitoring and logging effectively:

1. **Identify Requirements:** Understand the specific monitoring and logging requirements of your applications and infrastructure.
2. **Select Tools:** Choose appropriate monitoring and logging tools based on your requirements, technology stack, and budget.
3. **Define Metrics:** Define the key metrics and logs you need to capture to monitor the health and performance of your systems.
4. **Configure Alerts:** Set up alerts and notifications based on predefined thresholds to ensure timely responses to issues.
5. **Regularly Review and Tune:** Continuously review and refine your monitoring and logging configurations to ensure they remain effective as your system evolves.

Monitoring and logging are crucial aspects of maintaining a reliable and performant DevOps environment. They empower teams to proactively address issues, optimize performance, and enhance security, ultimately delivering a better user experience.

3.5 Evaluating and Selecting DevOps Tools

The DevOps landscape offers a plethora of tools and technologies to choose from, each catering to different aspects of the software development and delivery lifecycle. Evaluating and selecting the right DevOps tools is crucial for building an effective and efficient DevOps environment. In this section, we will discuss the factors to consider when evaluating and selecting DevOps tools and provide guidelines for making informed decisions.

Factors to Consider

1. Requirements and Goals

Begin by understanding your organization's specific requirements and DevOps goals. What problems are you trying to solve? What are your priorities, such as faster delivery, improved quality, or enhanced security?

2. Technology Stack

Consider your technology stack, including programming languages, databases, and infrastructure platforms. Some DevOps tools may be more compatible or feature-rich for certain technologies.

3. Integration Capabilities

Evaluate how well a tool can integrate with your existing toolchain. Integration with version control, CI/CD pipelines, monitoring, and logging tools is essential for a seamless workflow.

4. Scalability

Assess whether the tool can scale to accommodate the growth of your applications and infrastructure. Scalability is crucial for handling increased workloads.

5. Ease of Use

Consider the tool's user-friendliness and whether it requires extensive training or specialized skills to operate. An intuitive interface can accelerate adoption.

6. Community and Support

Examine the tool's community and support ecosystem. Active communities often result in frequent updates, plugins, and a wealth of resources for troubleshooting.

7. Cost

Evaluate the total cost of ownership, including licensing fees, infrastructure costs, and any hidden expenses. Some tools may offer free or open-source versions.

8. Security and Compliance

Ensure that the tool aligns with your security and compliance requirements. It should facilitate secure practices and compliance with industry standards.

Guidelines for Tool Selection

1. Define Selection Criteria

Establish clear selection criteria based on the factors mentioned above. Create a checklist of must-have features and capabilities.

2. Involve Stakeholders

Include representatives from development, operations, and other relevant teams in the decision-making process. Gather input on tool requirements and preferences.

3. Conduct Proof of Concept (PoC)

Perform a proof of concept with a shortlisted set of tools. Implement them in a controlled environment to assess their performance and compatibility.

4. Consider Long-Term Impact

Think about the long-term implications of tool selection. Will the tool be sustainable as your organization and infrastructure grow?

5. Evaluate Vendor Support

If considering commercial tools, assess the reputation and support capabilities of the vendors. Check for service-level agreements (SLAs) and customer reviews.

6. Seek Feedback

Seek feedback from other organizations or industry peers who have experience with the tools you are evaluating. Their insights can be valuable.

Example: Evaluating CI/CD Tools

Suppose you are evaluating CI/CD tools for your organization. Here are some considerations:

- **Integration:** Does the tool integrate well with your version control system (e.g., Git) and other DevOps tools like Jenkins or Travis CI?

- **Scalability:** Can the tool handle your expected workload, especially during peak times?

- **Ease of Use:** Is the user interface intuitive, and does it provide a smooth user experience for developers and operators?

- **Community and Support:** Is there an active community, and does the tool have good documentation and support resources?

- **Cost:** What is the pricing model, and does it fit within your budget constraints?

By systematically evaluating these factors and conducting a PoC, you can make an informed decision that aligns with your DevOps goals and requirements. Keep in mind that tool selection is not static; it should evolve as your organization's needs change and new tools emerge in the DevOps landscape.

Chapter 4: Continuous Integration and Deployment

4.1 The CI/CD Pipeline Explained

Continuous Integration and Continuous Deployment (CI/CD) are pivotal components of modern software development and DevOps practices. In this section, we will delve into the CI/CD pipeline, its significance, and the various stages that constitute it.

Understanding the CI/CD Pipeline

The CI/CD pipeline is a set of automated processes that streamline the building, testing, and deployment of software. It promotes collaboration among development, testing, and operations teams by ensuring that code changes are automatically integrated and delivered to production or staging environments. The CI/CD pipeline plays a vital role in achieving faster release cycles, higher code quality, and improved software delivery.

Key Stages of the CI/CD Pipeline

1. Code Commit

The CI/CD pipeline starts with a developer committing code changes to a version control system (e.g., Git). This step triggers the pipeline, initiating the automated workflow.

2. Code Build

In the code build stage, the pipeline automatically compiles the source code, compiles it into executable artifacts, and performs tasks such as dependency resolution.

3. Automated Testing

Automated testing is a critical phase of the pipeline. It includes unit tests, integration tests, and other forms of testing to ensure that the code changes do not introduce regressions or issues.

4. Artifact Generation

If all tests pass successfully, the pipeline generates deployable artifacts, which are typically binaries or container images. These artifacts represent the application's latest version.

5. Deployment

In the deployment stage, the pipeline automates the release process. It deploys the artifacts to the target environment, which can be a staging environment for further testing or the production environment for end-users.

6. Monitoring and Feedback

Continuous monitoring is essential for gathering insights into the application's performance and behavior. Metrics and logs are collected to identify issues, and feedback loops provide data for improvements.

7. Rollback (if necessary)

In the event of issues or failures in the production environment, automated rollback mechanisms can be triggered to revert to a previous stable version. This ensures minimal disruption to users.

Benefits of a CI/CD Pipeline

Implementing a CI/CD pipeline offers numerous advantages, including:

- **Faster Release Cycles:** CI/CD accelerates software delivery, enabling organizations to release updates and features more frequently.

- **Improved Code Quality:** Automated testing and validation reduce the likelihood of introducing bugs or regressions into the codebase.

- **Reduced Risk:** Automated deployments are less error-prone than manual deployments, leading to increased reliability and stability.

- **Collaboration:** CI/CD fosters collaboration among development, testing, and operations teams by automating and standardizing processes.

- **Efficiency:** Automation of repetitive tasks frees up time and resources for innovation and development.

CI/CD Tools

Several CI/CD tools are available, each with its strengths and features:

- **Jenkins:** An open-source automation server that supports building, deploying, and automating projects.

- **Travis CI:** A cloud-based CI/CD service that integrates seamlessly with version control systems like GitHub, making it easy to set up.

- **CircleCI:** Known for its scalability and flexibility, CircleCI automates the software development process.

- **GitLab CI/CD:** Tightly integrated with GitLab, it provides a complete DevOps platform with built-in CI/CD.

- **GitHub Actions:** GitHub's native CI/CD solution that enables developers to automate workflows directly within their GitHub repositories.

Each tool has its unique features and capabilities, and the choice depends on your organization's specific needs and preferences.

In summary, the CI/CD pipeline is a foundational practice in DevOps, streamlining the software delivery process from code commit to production deployment. It offers numerous benefits, including faster release cycles, improved code quality, and reduced risk. Selecting the right CI/CD tool and customizing your pipeline to align with your organization's goals are essential steps in achieving DevOps success.

4.2 Setting Up a Continuous Integration Environment

Setting up a Continuous Integration (CI) environment is a crucial step in modern software development practices. CI automates the process of code integration, ensuring that changes made by multiple developers do not introduce conflicts or defects. In this section, we will explore the key components and best practices for establishing an effective CI environment.

Key Components of a CI Environment

1. Version Control System (VCS)

A Version Control System (e.g., Git, SVN) is the foundation of CI. It allows developers to collaborate, track changes, and manage code repositories. VCS provides a centralized location for storing code and ensures that all changes are tracked.

2. CI Server/CI/CD Tool

A CI server or CI/CD tool automates the build and testing processes. Popular CI/CD tools like Jenkins, Travis CI, CircleCI, and GitLab CI/CD provide automation capabilities, integration with VCS, and reporting of build and test results.

3. Build Scripts

Build scripts (e.g., Makefile, Gradle, Maven) define how the application should be built from its source code. These scripts include commands for compiling code, resolving dependencies, and generating artifacts.

4. Automated Testing

Automated tests (unit, integration, and functional tests) are crucial in CI. These tests are executed automatically during the CI process to ensure that code changes do not introduce bugs or regressions.

5. Artifacts Repository

An artifacts repository (e.g., Nexus, Artifactory) stores built artifacts, such as compiled binaries or container images. These artifacts are used for deployment to various environments.

6. Notifications and Reporting

CI environments often include notifications and reporting features to inform developers and teams about the status of builds and tests. Email notifications, chat integrations, and dashboards are common tools for this purpose.

Best Practices for CI Setup

1. Use Version Control

Always use a version control system to manage code changes. Git is a widely adopted choice, offering branching, merging, and collaboration capabilities.

2. Automate Builds

Automate the build process using build scripts or build automation tools. This ensures consistency and repeatability in the build process.

3. Implement Automated Testing

Integrate automated testing into your CI pipeline. This includes unit tests, integration tests, and any other relevant test types. Failing tests should prevent code from being merged.

4. Isolate Dependencies

Isolate dependencies to prevent conflicts and ensure reproducibility. Use tools like package managers (e.g., npm, pip, Maven) to manage dependencies.

5. Parallelize Builds and Tests

Parallelize builds and tests to reduce build times. CI tools often support parallel execution of jobs across multiple machines or containers.

6. Use a Dedicated CI Server/Tool

Utilize a dedicated CI server or CI/CD tool rather than running CI on developer machines. This ensures consistency and automation.

7. Continuous Integration, Not Continuous Delivery

Differentiate between CI and Continuous Delivery (CD). CI focuses on code integration and automated testing, while CD includes automated deployment to production.

8. Implement CI/CD Pipelines

Create CI/CD pipelines that include stages for building, testing, and deploying code. Ensure that deployment to production is a controlled and separate stage.

Example CI Configuration (Jenkinsfile)

Here is an example Jenkinsfile, a configuration file used in Jenkins for defining CI/CD pipelines:

```
pipeline {

agent any

stages {

stage('Checkout') {

steps {

// Checkout code from version control

checkout scm

}

}

stage('Build') {

steps {

// Build the application (e.g., using Maven)

sh 'mvn clean package'

}
```

```
}

stage('Test') {

steps {

// Run automated tests

sh 'mvn test'

}

}

stage('Deploy to Staging') {

steps {

// Deploy to a staging environment

sh 'kubectl apply -f staging.yaml'

}

}

}

}
```

This Jenkinsfile defines a basic CI/CD pipeline with stages for code checkout, building, testing, and deploying to a staging environment. Jenkins executes these stages automatically upon code changes.

Setting up a robust CI environment with the right tools and best practices is essential for achieving efficient and reliable software development processes. It enhances collaboration, accelerates the identification of issues, and ensures that only high-quality code is integrated into the project.

4.3 Best Practices for Continuous Deployment

Continuous Deployment (CD) is a vital aspect of DevOps, enabling the automated and continuous delivery of code changes to production environments. While it offers numerous benefits, implementing CD requires careful planning and adherence to best practices to ensure the stability and reliability of the production environment. In this section, we will explore key best practices for continuous deployment.

1. Automate Everything

Automation is the cornerstone of continuous deployment. Automate the entire deployment process, from code integration and testing to deployment itself. This reduces the chance of human error and ensures consistency.

2. Implement Continuous Integration First

Before diving into continuous deployment, establish a solid continuous integration (CI) process. CI involves automatically integrating code changes, running tests, and providing rapid feedback. CD builds upon a successful CI foundation.

3. Small, Frequent Releases

Opt for small, incremental releases rather than large, infrequent ones. Smaller releases are easier to manage and troubleshoot if issues arise. They also allow for quicker feedback and course correction.

4. Blue-Green Deployments

Implement blue-green deployments or canary releases to minimize risk. Blue-green deployments involve running two parallel environments: one with the current version (blue) and one with the new version (green). This allows for immediate rollback in case of issues.

5. Rollback Plans

Always have rollback plans in place. Despite rigorous testing, issues can still occur in production. Knowing how to roll back to a previous version quickly is essential to minimize downtime and user impact.

6. Feature Flags and Toggles

Use feature flags or toggles to enable or disable specific features in production. This allows you to release unfinished or experimental features to a subset of users and gradually enable them for everyone when ready.

7. Immutable Infrastructure

Adopt immutable infrastructure practices where servers and environments are treated as disposable and are recreated from scratch with each deployment. This reduces drift and ensures consistency.

8. Automated Testing at All Stages

Include automated tests at every stage of the deployment pipeline. This includes unit tests, integration tests, regression tests, and security tests. Automated tests provide confidence in the quality of the code being deployed.

9. Monitoring and Alerts

Implement robust monitoring and alerting systems to track the health and performance of your production environment. Set up alerts for key metrics and be proactive in addressing issues.

10. Security as Code

Incorporate security practices into your CD pipeline. Perform automated security scans and vulnerability assessments as part of the deployment process. Security should not be an afterthought.

11. Documentation and Runbooks

Maintain detailed documentation and runbooks for your applications and infrastructure. These documents should provide instructions on troubleshooting common issues and performing routine maintenance tasks.

12. Collaboration and Communication

Foster collaboration and communication between development, operations, and other teams involved in the CD process. Clear communication channels and shared responsibilities are crucial.

13. Testing in Production

Consider implementing testing in production by directing a small percentage of real user traffic to the new version. This provides valuable insights into how the application behaves in the production environment.

14. Immutable Artifact Repositories

Store artifacts in immutable artifact repositories. Once an artifact is built, it should not change. This ensures that the same artifact is deployed to all environments.

15. Continuous Feedback and Improvement

Continuously collect feedback from users and stakeholders. Use this feedback to drive improvements in the CD process and the application itself.

16. Disaster Recovery Plans

Develop and test disaster recovery plans. These plans outline steps to take in the event of catastrophic failures to minimize downtime and data loss.

17. Compliance and Auditing

If your organization has compliance requirements, ensure that your CD process aligns with these regulations. Maintain audit trails and documentation as necessary.

Successful continuous deployment requires a combination of automation, testing, monitoring, and careful planning. By following these best practices, organizations can achieve faster delivery, higher quality, and improved agility in their software development and deployment processes while maintaining the stability of their production environments.

4.4 Handling Rollbacks and Failures

In the world of continuous deployment (CD), where code changes are automatically delivered to production, it's essential to have robust strategies in place for handling rollbacks and failures. Despite the best testing and automation practices, issues can still arise. This section discusses how to gracefully handle failures and execute rollbacks when necessary.

Rollback Strategies

1. Blue-Green Rollbacks

If you've implemented a blue-green deployment strategy, rollbacks become more manageable. Simply switch traffic back to the previous (blue) environment if issues arise with the new (green) version. Blue-green deployments are a powerful tool for minimizing downtime during rollbacks.

2. Rollback Deployments

Maintain rollback deployments as part of your CD pipeline. For each deployment, create an equivalent rollback deployment that reverts the environment to the previous state. This ensures that you can quickly return to a known good state.

3. Database Migrations

If your application involves database changes, use database migration tools and scripts that are backward-compatible. This allows you to roll back to the previous database schema and data if needed.

4. Feature Flags

Feature flags or toggles can be a lifesaver during rollbacks. If a new feature causes issues, you can simply disable it using feature flags, instantly reverting to the previous behavior.

Monitoring and Alerting

1. Real-time Monitoring

Implement real-time monitoring of your production environment. This includes monitoring server health, application performance, and user behavior. Monitoring helps identify issues as they occur.

2. Alerting

Set up alerting systems to notify your operations team immediately when critical issues are detected. Alerts should be actionable and provide enough context to diagnose and resolve problems quickly.

3. Escalation Policies

Define escalation policies that specify how alerts should be handled. These policies ensure that alerts are not ignored and are addressed promptly, even during off-hours.

Incident Response

1. Incident Management

Establish an incident management process that outlines how incidents are reported, tracked, and resolved. Define roles and responsibilities within the incident response team.

2. Severity Levels

Categorize incidents by severity levels. High-severity incidents require immediate attention and may trigger a rollback, while lower-severity incidents can be addressed during normal work hours.

3. Post-Incident Analysis

After resolving an incident, conduct a post-mortem or post-incident analysis. Identify the root cause, document lessons learned, and update procedures to prevent similar issues in the future.

Rollback Testing

1. Automated Rollback Testing

Include automated rollback testing as part of your CD pipeline. Ensure that the rollback process is tested regularly to verify that it works as expected.

2. Partial Rollback Testing

Test partial rollbacks for applications with multiple components. Verify that you can selectively roll back specific parts of the application without affecting the entire system.

Communication

1. Internal Communication

Maintain clear and open communication channels within your organization. Ensure that all relevant teams are informed of incidents and rollbacks.

2. External Communication

If a rollback affects end-users or customers, communicate transparently about the situation, the actions being taken, and the expected resolution timeline. Manage user expectations and provide updates as needed.

Continuous Improvement

1. Learning from Failures

Use incidents and rollbacks as learning opportunities. Analyze the causes of failures and develop strategies to prevent similar issues in the future. Implement improvements iteratively.

2. Documentation Updates

Keep incident response and rollback procedures up to date. As your systems evolve, ensure that your documentation reflects the current state of your environment and processes.

Handling rollbacks and failures gracefully is an integral part of maintaining a robust continuous deployment process. By implementing rollback strategies, effective monitoring and alerting, incident response procedures, rollback testing, and clear communication, organizations can minimize downtime, reduce the impact of issues, and continuously improve their CD practices.

4.5 Case Studies: Effective CI/CD Implementation

In this section, we will explore a few real-world case studies that showcase the effective implementation of Continuous Integration and Continuous Deployment (CI/CD) practices. These examples highlight the benefits, challenges, and outcomes of CI/CD adoption in different organizations.

Case Study 1: Netflix

Background: Netflix, a global streaming platform, relies heavily on its online service to deliver content to millions of users worldwide. They need to continuously update their platform with new features and improvements while maintaining high availability.

CI/CD Implementation: Netflix has a robust CI/CD pipeline in place that enables them to deploy changes to their production environment frequently. They use a canary deployment strategy, where a small percentage of users receive new features first. If no issues are detected, the feature is gradually rolled out to all users.

Benefits: Netflix's CI/CD practices allow them to release updates and fixes rapidly. They can experiment with new features without risking the entire user base's experience. The ability to roll back quickly in case of issues minimizes disruptions.

Challenges: Managing such a large-scale CI/CD pipeline is complex. Ensuring the stability of the service while making frequent changes is a significant challenge. Netflix invests heavily in automation and monitoring to address these challenges.

Case Study 2: Etsy

Background: Etsy, an online marketplace for handmade and vintage items, focuses on empowering sellers and providing a smooth shopping experience. They needed a CI/CD approach to improve their release process.

CI/CD Implementation: Etsy embraced CI/CD to automate their deployment process. They implemented feature flags to control the release of new features and performed extensive automated testing. Code changes go through multiple stages of testing before reaching production.

Benefits: Etsy achieved faster releases with reduced manual intervention. Feature flags allow them to roll out changes selectively, ensuring that they can quickly respond to user feedback and issues. This approach also minimizes the blast radius of potential problems.

Challenges: Implementing CI/CD required significant cultural and organizational changes. Teams had to adapt to the new way of working, emphasizing automation and collaboration. Ensuring the reliability of the CI/CD pipeline was also a challenge.

Case Study 3: Amazon

Background: Amazon, one of the world's largest e-commerce and cloud computing companies, relies on a robust CI/CD pipeline to support its diverse services and platforms.

CI/CD Implementation: Amazon's CI/CD pipeline is highly automated and integrated with its cloud services. They use blue-green deployments to minimize downtime during releases. Amazon places a strong emphasis on testing, including load testing and security testing.

Benefits: Amazon's CI/CD practices allow them to continuously improve their services and rapidly respond to customer needs. They can release updates to their vast infrastructure with minimal disruption.

Challenges: Managing a massive and complex CI/CD pipeline across various services is a significant challenge. Ensuring that security and compliance requirements are met at scale is another ongoing challenge.

These case studies demonstrate the diverse applications of CI/CD practices across different industries and organizations. While the specific implementations and challenges vary, the common thread is the emphasis on automation, testing, and frequent, incremental releases to deliver high-quality software and services to end-users.

Chapter 5: Testing in a DevOps World

5.1 Importance of Automated Testing

Automated testing is a fundamental practice in DevOps that plays a pivotal role in ensuring the quality, reliability, and stability of software applications throughout their development lifecycle. In this section, we will explore the significance of automated testing and its various aspects within the DevOps framework.

Benefits of Automated Testing

1. Early Detection of Issues

Automated tests can be executed continuously throughout the development process, catching issues at an early stage. This early detection reduces the cost and effort required to fix problems and minimizes the chances of defects reaching production.

2. Rapid Feedback

Automated tests provide rapid feedback to developers. When a code change breaks existing functionality or introduces regressions, tests immediately notify the development team. This quick feedback loop allows for prompt resolution.

3. Consistency

Automated tests are consistent in their execution. They perform the same set of tests every time, eliminating human variability. Consistency ensures that tests are reliable indicators of code quality.

4. Regression Testing

As software evolves, new features and changes can inadvertently impact existing functionality. Automated tests excel at regression testing, ensuring that existing features continue to work as intended after code changes.

5. Efficiency

Automated testing is more efficient than manual testing. It can run a large number of test cases in a fraction of the time it would take a human tester. This efficiency is especially valuable in fast-paced DevOps environments.

Types of Automated Testing

1. Unit Testing

Unit tests focus on testing individual components or functions in isolation. They verify that each unit of code (e.g., a function or class) behaves correctly. Unit tests are the foundation of automated testing.

2. Integration Testing

Integration tests examine how different components or services interact with each other. They ensure that integrated parts of the application work together seamlessly.

3. Functional Testing

Functional tests evaluate the application's functionality from an end-user perspective. They test scenarios and workflows to confirm that the software meets its intended requirements.

4. Performance Testing

Performance testing assesses the application's responsiveness, scalability, and resource usage under various conditions. It helps identify bottlenecks and optimize system performance.

5. Security Testing

Security testing focuses on identifying vulnerabilities and security weaknesses in the application. It includes activities like penetration testing, code analysis, and vulnerability scanning.

Test Automation Frameworks

1. JUnit (Java)

JUnit is a popular unit testing framework for Java. It provides annotations and libraries for writing and executing unit tests.

2. pytest (Python)

pytest is a testing framework for Python that simplifies test discovery and execution. It supports various types of testing, including unit, integration, and functional testing.

3. Selenium

Selenium is a widely used framework for automating web application testing. It allows testers to automate interactions with web browsers to perform functional testing.

4. Jenkins

Jenkins, a popular CI/CD tool, includes built-in support for running automated tests as part of the CI pipeline. It can trigger test execution and report results.

Test Driven Development (TDD)

Test Driven Development (TDD) is a software development approach that emphasizes writing tests before writing code. Developers define test cases based on expected functionality and then implement code to make the tests pass. TDD ensures that code is thoroughly tested and meets requirements from the outset.

Automated testing is an integral component of DevOps, enabling teams to release software quickly and confidently. It provides numerous benefits, including early issue detection, rapid feedback, consistency, and efficiency. By employing various types of automated tests and utilizing test automation frameworks, organizations can maintain high-quality software while keeping pace with the demands of modern software development.

5.2 Integration and Functional Testing Strategies

Integration and functional testing are critical aspects of automated testing in DevOps, focusing on ensuring that the various components of a software application work together seamlessly and meet functional requirements. In this section, we will delve into strategies and best practices for conducting effective integration and functional testing within the DevOps framework.

Integration Testing

1. Test Data Isolation

Isolate test data from production data to maintain a clean and controlled testing environment. Avoid using production data for testing, as it may contain sensitive information and could lead to unintentional data modifications.

2. Use of Mocks and Stubs

Incorporate mocks and stubs to simulate the behavior of external dependencies, such as databases or APIs, during integration testing. This allows you to focus on testing the interaction between components without relying on external systems.

3. Test in Realistic Environments

Conduct integration tests in environments that closely mimic production settings. Ensure that configurations, network conditions, and other variables align with those in the production environment to identify potential issues accurately.

4. Continuous Integration

Integrate integration tests into your Continuous Integration (CI) pipeline. Automate the execution of integration tests whenever code changes are pushed, providing rapid feedback to developers.

5. Regression Testing

Perform regular regression testing to verify that recent code changes have not negatively impacted existing integrations. A well-maintained suite of regression tests helps detect integration issues early.

Functional Testing

1. Requirements-Based Testing

Align functional tests with the application's requirements and specifications. Functional tests should cover the expected behavior of features and functionalities as defined in user stories and documentation.

2. Boundary Value Analysis

Conduct boundary value analysis to test extreme values and edge cases. This ensures that the application behaves correctly near its boundaries, helping identify issues related to data limits or constraints.

3. Equivalence Partitioning

Apply equivalence partitioning to group similar inputs into test cases. This technique helps reduce the number of test cases while ensuring that each group is adequately tested. For example, testing different age ranges for user registration.

4. Exploratory Testing

Complement automated functional tests with exploratory testing performed by human testers. Exploratory testing allows testers to explore the application, uncover unexpected issues, and assess usability and user experience.

5. Cross-Browser and Cross-Device Testing

In cases where the application targets multiple browsers and devices, conduct functional testing across various combinations to ensure compatibility and consistent functionality.

Test Automation Tools

1. Selenium

Selenium is a widely used tool for automating web application testing. It supports the creation of automated scripts for browser-based functional testing.

2. Postman

Postman is a popular tool for API testing. It allows testers to create and execute automated tests for RESTful APIs, making it essential for integration testing.

3. Junit and TestNG

JUnit and TestNG are widely used testing frameworks for Java applications. They facilitate the creation and execution of unit, integration, and functional tests.

4. Cypress

Cypress is a JavaScript-based end-to-end testing framework that focuses on ensuring the functionality and behavior of web applications.

5. Cucumber

Cucumber is a tool that supports Behavior-Driven Development (BDD) and allows the creation of readable and executable functional tests using natural language.

Continuous Monitoring

1. Real-Time Monitoring

Implement real-time monitoring of application components during integration and functional testing. Monitoring tools can alert teams to issues as they occur, facilitating immediate resolution.

2. Performance Metrics

Capture performance metrics during functional testing, such as response times and resource utilization. These metrics help assess the application's efficiency and scalability.

3. Logging and Error Handling

Enhance error handling and logging mechanisms to provide detailed information when functional tests fail. Detailed logs aid in debugging and identifying the root cause of issues.

Effective integration and functional testing are essential for validating that software applications meet functional requirements and operate seamlessly. By following best practices, leveraging automation tools, and incorporating continuous monitoring, organizations can ensure the reliability and quality of their software, enabling them to deliver value to users with confidence in the DevOps pipeline.

5.3 Performance Testing in Continuous Delivery

Performance testing is a crucial aspect of ensuring that a software application can handle the expected load and maintain acceptable performance levels under various conditions. In the context of Continuous Delivery (CD), performance testing becomes even more critical, as it helps identify performance bottlenecks early in the development process. In this section, we will explore the importance of performance testing in CD and discuss various strategies and types of performance testing.

Importance of Performance Testing in CD

1. Early Detection of Performance Issues

Performance testing in the CD pipeline allows teams to detect and address performance issues during the development phase. Early detection reduces the cost and effort required to fix such issues when compared to identifying them in production.

2. Optimization and Scalability

Performance testing provides insights into the application's scalability. It helps determine how the application behaves as the user load increases, allowing organizations to optimize their infrastructure and resources accordingly.

3. User Experience

Ensuring good performance is essential for providing a positive user experience. Slow-loading web pages or unresponsive applications can lead to user frustration and abandonment.

4. Cost Savings

By identifying and resolving performance bottlenecks early, organizations can avoid the potential costs associated with downtime, user loss, and emergency fixes in production.

Types of Performance Testing

1. Load Testing

Load testing assesses how the application performs under expected load conditions. It helps determine the maximum capacity the system can handle before performance degrades.

2. Stress Testing

Stress testing goes beyond load testing by evaluating the application's behavior under extreme conditions. It helps identify breaking points and weaknesses in the system.

3. Scalability Testing

Scalability testing assesses how well the application can scale vertically (adding more resources to a single server) and horizontally (adding more servers) to accommodate increased load.

4. Endurance Testing

Endurance testing evaluates the application's performance over an extended period to identify issues related to resource leaks, memory consumption, and degradation over time.

5. Spike Testing

Spike testing simulates sudden and extreme increases in user load to assess how the application handles unexpected traffic spikes.

Strategies for Performance Testing in CD

1. Automate Performance Tests

Integrate performance tests into your CD pipeline and automate their execution. Automating tests ensures consistency and enables frequent testing without manual intervention.

2. Use Realistic Scenarios

Create performance test scenarios that closely mimic real-world usage patterns. Consider factors like user behavior, data volume, and peak traffic times.

3. Continuous Monitoring

Implement continuous monitoring of application performance during the testing process. Monitor key metrics such as response times, resource utilization, and error rates.

4. Test Data Management

Manage test data effectively to ensure that performance tests are conducted with relevant and representative data. Avoid using synthetic or outdated data for testing.

5. Collaborate Across Teams

Performance testing should involve collaboration between development, testing, and operations teams. It helps ensure that performance issues are addressed comprehensively.

Performance Testing Tools

1. Apache JMeter

Apache JMeter is a widely used open-source tool for load testing and performance testing. It supports various protocols and provides extensive reporting capabilities.

2. Gatling

Gatling is an open-source load testing tool that uses Scala for scripting. It is designed for creating realistic and scalable performance tests.

3. Locust

Locust is an open-source Python-based load testing tool. It allows you to write test scenarios as code, making it highly customizable.

4. New Relic

New Relic is a performance monitoring platform that provides real-time insights into application performance. It helps identify performance bottlenecks in production.

5. Dynatrace

Dynatrace is an application performance monitoring tool that offers AI-driven insights into application performance, user experience, and infrastructure.

Performance testing is an integral part of the CD process, ensuring that applications meet performance expectations and can handle increased load. By implementing performance testing strategies, leveraging appropriate tools, and fostering collaboration across teams, organizations can deliver high-performance applications that provide a positive user experience and minimize the risk of performance-related issues in production.

5.4 Security Testing in the DevOps Process

Security testing is an integral part of the DevOps process, known as DevSecOps, which emphasizes integrating security practices into the entire software development lifecycle. It aims to identify and mitigate security vulnerabilities and risks early in the development process, reducing the likelihood of security breaches and data breaches in production. In this section, we will explore the significance of security testing in DevOps and discuss various security testing types and best practices.

Importance of Security Testing in DevOps

1. Early Vulnerability Detection

Integrating security testing into the DevOps pipeline allows organizations to identify and address security vulnerabilities at an early stage of development. This reduces the potential impact and cost of addressing security issues after deployment.

2. Compliance and Regulations

Many industries have specific security and compliance requirements, such as GDPR, HIPAA, or PCI DSS. DevSecOps practices help organizations ensure compliance by continuously testing and monitoring security controls.

3. Risk Mitigation

Identifying and mitigating security risks proactively helps organizations reduce the risk of security breaches, data leaks, and reputational damage.

4. Secure Code Development

DevSecOps encourages secure coding practices, making it easier for developers to write secure code from the beginning. It includes secure coding guidelines, threat modeling, and code analysis.

Types of Security Testing

1. Static Application Security Testing (SAST)

SAST analyzes source code, bytecode, or binary code to identify security vulnerabilities. It scans the code for known security issues, such as SQL injection, cross-site scripting (XSS), and insecure configurations.

2. Dynamic Application Security Testing (DAST)

DAST assesses a running application from the outside by sending various inputs and payloads to identify vulnerabilities and weaknesses. It simulates real-world attacks, making it valuable for testing production environments.

3. Interactive Application Security Testing (IAST)

IAST combines aspects of SAST and DAST by monitoring the application during runtime and analyzing the code. It provides real-time feedback on vulnerabilities and their context.

4. Software Composition Analysis (SCA)

SCA identifies security vulnerabilities in third-party libraries and components used in an application. It helps organizations track and manage open-source dependencies and their associated security risks.

5. Container Security Scanning

Container security scanning focuses on identifying vulnerabilities in container images. It ensures that containers used in DevOps environments are free from known vulnerabilities.

Best Practices for Security Testing in DevOps

1. Shift Left

Shift security left in the development process by integrating security practices from the initial design and coding phases. This approach ensures that security is considered at every stage of development.

2. Automate Security Tests

Automate security tests to ensure consistent and repeatable assessments. Integrate security testing tools into the CI/CD pipeline to identify vulnerabilities in code changes automatically.

3. Threat Modeling

Use threat modeling techniques to identify potential security threats and attack vectors in the application's design and architecture. Address these threats during development.

4. Penetration Testing

Conduct regular penetration testing to simulate real-world attacks on the application. Penetration tests help identify vulnerabilities that automated tools might miss.

5. Security Training

Provide security training and awareness programs for development and operations teams. Ensure that team members understand secure coding practices and security risks.

6. Vulnerability Management

Implement a vulnerability management process to track and remediate identified security vulnerabilities promptly. Prioritize vulnerabilities based on severity and risk.

7. Continuous Monitoring

Implement continuous security monitoring to detect and respond to security incidents in real-time. Use security information and event management (SIEM) systems for monitoring.

Security testing is essential in DevOps to protect applications and data from security threats. By integrating security testing into the

DevOps process, organizations can identify vulnerabilities early, reduce risks, and build secure software. DevSecOps practices, when followed diligently, help create a culture of security awareness and collaboration across development, testing, and operations teams.

5.5 Maintaining Quality While Accelerating Releases

Maintaining software quality while accelerating the release cycle is a primary challenge in DevOps. Organizations aim to deliver software faster while ensuring that it meets quality standards and customer expectations. In this section, we will explore strategies and best practices for maintaining and even enhancing software quality in a DevOps environment.

Quality Assurance in DevOps

1. Shift-Left Testing

Shift-left testing involves moving testing activities earlier in the development cycle. Developers are encouraged to write unit tests, conduct code reviews, and perform static analysis to catch issues before they propagate further in the pipeline.

2. Continuous Testing

Continuous testing is an essential practice in DevOps. It involves automating tests at various stages of the pipeline, including unit, integration, functional, and performance testing. Automated tests provide rapid feedback and enable early issue detection.

3. Parallel Testing

Parallel testing involves running multiple tests concurrently to reduce testing time. By leveraging cloud resources and containerization, teams can perform parallel testing to expedite the testing process.

4. Test Data Management

Effective test data management ensures that tests are conducted with relevant and representative data. It involves creating and maintaining data sets that mimic production scenarios.

Code Quality and Review

1. Code Reviews

Code reviews are crucial for maintaining code quality. Peer reviews help identify issues, ensure adherence to coding standards, and promote knowledge sharing among team members.

2. Static Code Analysis

Static code analysis tools automatically analyze code for potential issues, such as code smells, security vulnerabilities, and adherence to coding standards. These tools provide developers with actionable insights to improve code quality.

Monitoring and Observability

1. Real-Time Monitoring

Implement real-time monitoring and observability in production environments. Continuous monitoring allows teams to detect and respond to issues promptly, improving application reliability.

2. Logging and Error Handling

Enhance logging and error handling mechanisms to capture relevant information when issues occur in production. Detailed logs aid in diagnosing and resolving issues quickly.

Deployment Strategies

1. Blue-Green Deployments

Blue-green deployments involve maintaining two identical environments, one for the current production version (blue) and one for the new version (green). This approach allows for seamless and risk-free deployments by switching traffic between the environments.

2. Canary Releases

Canary releases involve deploying new features or changes to a small subset of users or servers first. This allows organizations to gather real-world feedback and detect issues before a full release.

Infrastructure as Code (IaC)

1. Automate Infrastructure

Use Infrastructure as Code (IaC) to automate the provisioning and configuration of infrastructure. IaC ensures consistency, repeatability, and traceability of infrastructure changes.

2. Version Control for Infrastructure

Treat infrastructure code as part of your application code and manage it in version control systems. This enables teams to track changes, collaborate, and roll back to previous configurations if needed.

Collaboration and Communication

1. Cross-Functional Collaboration

Encourage collaboration and communication among development, testing, and operations teams. Cross-functional teams are better equipped to address issues and make informed decisions collectively.

2. Feedback Loops

Establish feedback loops to continuously gather input from users, stakeholders, and the development team. Feedback drives improvements and ensures that software aligns with user expectations.

Continuous Improvement

1. Retrospectives

Conduct regular retrospectives to reflect on the DevOps process and identify areas for improvement. Retrospectives enable teams to adapt and evolve their practices.

2. Metrics and KPIs

Define and monitor key performance indicators (KPIs) related to quality, release cycles, and user satisfaction. Data-driven insights help teams make informed decisions and track progress.

Maintaining and enhancing software quality in DevOps is achievable through a combination of practices, tools, and a culture of continuous improvement. By shifting testing left, automating tests, optimizing code quality, and fostering collaboration, organizations can deliver high-quality software at an accelerated pace. Monitoring and feedback mechanisms, along with deployment strategies like blue-green and canary releases, further enhance the ability to maintain quality while releasing software faster.

Chapter 6: Infrastructure as Code (IaC)

6.1 Introduction to IaC

Infrastructure as Code (IaC) is a fundamental concept in the world of DevOps and modern software development. It refers to the practice of managing and provisioning infrastructure using code and automation scripts rather than manual processes. In this section, we will delve into the key principles, benefits, and techniques associated with Infrastructure as Code.

The Need for IaC

Traditional infrastructure management involves manual provisioning and configuration of servers, networks, and other resources. This manual approach is not only time-consuming but also error-prone, leading to inconsistencies and operational challenges. IaC emerged as a solution to address these issues by treating infrastructure components as code.

Key Principles of IaC

IaC is based on several core principles:

1. **Declarative Configuration**: IaC uses declarative scripts to define the desired state of infrastructure. It focuses on what the infrastructure should look like rather than specifying step-by-step instructions.
2. **Version Control**: IaC code should be stored in version control systems (e.g., Git) to track changes, collaborate with teams, and ensure version history.
3. **Automation**: Automation is at the heart of IaC. Scripts and templates automate the provisioning, configuration,

and management of infrastructure components.

4. **Idempotency**: IaC scripts should be idempotent, meaning that running them multiple times produces the same result as running them once. This ensures consistency and repeatability.

5. **Modularity**: IaC encourages breaking down infrastructure into smaller, manageable modules or components that can be reused across different projects.

Benefits of IaC

Implementing Infrastructure as Code offers several advantages:

- **Scalability**: IaC allows you to scale infrastructure up or down as needed, making it easier to handle changes in workload.

- **Consistency**: IaC ensures that your infrastructure is consistent across environments, reducing configuration drift and errors.

- **Efficiency**: Automation through IaC reduces the time and effort required for provisioning and maintenance.

- **Collaboration**: Version control and collaboration tools enable teams to work together on infrastructure code.

- **Disaster Recovery**: IaC facilitates disaster recovery by recreating infrastructure quickly from code.

Tools for IaC

There are various tools and frameworks available for implementing IaC, including:

- **Terraform**: A widely-used open-source tool for building, changing, and versioning infrastructure efficiently.

- **AWS CloudFormation**: Amazon's service for defining and deploying AWS infrastructure as code.

- **Ansible**: A configuration management tool that can also be used for IaC.

- **Chef and Puppet**: Configuration management tools that can manage infrastructure as code alongside application configurations.

Getting Started with IaC

To get started with IaC, you'll need to choose a tool that fits your needs and infrastructure provider. Then, you can begin writing code to describe your infrastructure. Start with a small project to learn and experiment with IaC principles and best practices.

In the following sections of this chapter, we will explore the tools, techniques, and best practices for implementing Infrastructure as Code effectively, helping you streamline and automate your infrastructure management.

6.2 Tools for Infrastructure Automation

When it comes to Infrastructure as Code (IaC), selecting the right tools and automation frameworks is crucial. In this section, we will explore some of the prominent tools and technologies commonly used for infrastructure automation in DevOps practices.

1. Terraform

Terraform[1] is one of the most popular open-source IaC tools. Developed by HashiCorp, Terraform allows you to define infrastructure components as code using a domain-specific language (DSL). It supports various cloud providers, including AWS, Azure, Google Cloud, and more. Terraform's strength lies in its declarative syntax, enabling you to describe the desired state of your infrastructure and allowing Terraform to plan and apply changes.

Example Terraform code to create an AWS EC2 instance:

```
resource "aws_instance" "example" {

ami = "ami-0c55b159cbfafe1f0"

instance_type = "t2.micro"

}
```

2. AWS CloudFormation

AWS CloudFormation is Amazon's native IaC service. It provides templates for defining and provisioning AWS infrastructure resources. CloudFormation templates are written in JSON or YAML and can describe a wide range of AWS resources, such as EC2 instances, S3 buckets, and RDS databases.

Example CloudFormation template snippet to create an S3 bucket:

```
{

"Resources": {

"MyS3Bucket": {
```

---

1. https://www.terraform.io/

```
"Type": "AWS::S3::Bucket",

"Properties": {

"BucketName": "my-unique-bucket-name"

}

}

}

}
```

3. Ansible

Ansible[2] is a powerful automation tool that can be used for both configuration management and IaC. Ansible uses YAML-based playbooks to define tasks, and it can manage infrastructure across various cloud providers, on-premises data centers, and network devices. Ansible is agentless and relies on SSH or PowerShell for communication with target hosts.

Example Ansible playbook to install and configure Nginx:

—-

```
- name: Install and configure Nginx

hosts: web_servers

tasks:

- name: Install Nginx

apt:
```

```
name: nginx

state: present

- name: Copy Nginx config

copy:

src: /path/to/nginx.conf

dest: /etc/nginx/nginx.conf

- name: Start Nginx service

service:

name: nginx

state: started
```

4. Puppet and Chef

Puppet[3] and Chef[4] are widely used configuration management tools that can also be employed for IaC purposes. They use Ruby-based DSLs to define infrastructure configurations and can manage not only software installations but also the underlying infrastructure. Puppet and Chef are suitable for enterprises with complex infrastructure needs.

Example Puppet manifest to manage a package and service:

```
package { 'apache2':

ensure => 'installed',

}
```

---

3. https://puppet.com/

4. https://www.chef.io/

```
service { 'apache2':

ensure => 'running',

enable => true,

}
```

5. Pulumi

Pulumi[5] is a relatively new IaC tool that takes a modern approach by using familiar programming languages like JavaScript, Python, and Go to define infrastructure. This allows developers to leverage their existing skills and libraries while creating infrastructure as code. Pulumi supports multiple cloud providers and offers a unique approach to managing cloud resources.

Example Pulumi code to create an Azure storage account:

```
const { azure } = require("@pulumi/azure");

const storageAccount = new azure.storage.Account("storage", {

resourceGroupName: "myResourceGroup",

accountReplicationType: "LRS",

accountTier: "Standard",

});
```

These are just a few examples of the many tools available for infrastructure automation in DevOps. The choice of tool depends on factors like your team's familiarity with a specific tool, your infrastructure provider, and the complexity of your infrastructure.

---

5. https://www.pulumi.com/

Whichever tool you choose, the goal remains the same: to streamline and automate the management of your infrastructure through code.

6.3 Managing Configuration as Code

In the realm of Infrastructure as Code (IaC), managing configuration as code is a critical aspect. Configuration as code involves defining and maintaining configuration settings for various software components and services in a version-controlled manner. This section delves into the significance of managing configuration as code and best practices associated with it.

Why Manage Configuration as Code?

Configuration as code is essential for several reasons:

1. **Reproducibility**: Storing configuration as code ensures that your infrastructure and applications can be recreated exactly as they were at a specific point in time. This reproducibility is crucial for debugging and disaster recovery.

2. **Collaboration**: Configuration code can be version-controlled, allowing teams to collaborate effectively, track changes, and review configurations before deployment.

3. **Automation**: Configuration code can be automatically applied during deployment, reducing manual configuration tasks and the risk of human errors.

4. **Consistency**: Managing configuration as code ensures that all instances of a service or application share the same configuration, reducing configuration drift and inconsistencies.

Best Practices for Managing Configuration as Code

To effectively manage configuration as code, consider the following best practices:

1. **Version Control**: Store configuration files in a version control system (e.g., Git) to track changes, manage versions, and enable collaboration.

2. **Separate Configuration from Code**: Keep configuration separate from application code. This allows for easier updates and reduces the complexity of code repositories.

3. **Environment-specific Configurations**: Use environment-specific configuration files or variables to adapt configurations for different environments (e.g., development, staging, production).

4. **Parameterization**: Parameterize configurations to make them flexible and reusable. Use placeholders or variables for environment-specific values.

5. **Immutable Infrastructure**: Aim for immutable infrastructure, where changes to configuration result in the creation of a new instance rather than modifying existing instances.

6. **Secret Management**: Handle sensitive information (e.g., API keys, passwords) separately from code. Use secure vaults or secret management tools to store and retrieve secrets.

7. **Testing**: Implement automated testing of configuration changes to ensure they don't introduce errors or vulnerabilities.

8. **Documentation**: Maintain documentation for configurations, including descriptions of variables, their purpose, and their valid values.

Examples of Configuration as Code

1. **Docker Compose**: Docker Compose allows you to define application services, networks, and volumes in a YAML file, making it easy to manage containerized applications' configurations.

version: '3'

services:

web:

image: nginx:latest

ports:

- "80:80"

1. **Spring Boot Configuration**: In Java applications developed using Spring Boot, configuration settings can be externalized in properties or YAML files and accessed using annotations.

@Value("${app.apiKey}")

private String apiKey;

1. **Terraform Variables**: Terraform allows you to define variables for configurations, making it possible to customize infrastructure deployments for different environments.

variable "region" {

description = "AWS region"

```
type = string

default = "us-west-2"

}
```

Managing configuration as code is a fundamental practice in modern software development and DevOps. It enhances the reliability, repeatability, and scalability of infrastructure and applications, ensuring that they remain consistent across different environments and reducing operational complexities.

6.4 Version Control for Infrastructure

In the world of DevOps and Infrastructure as Code (IaC), version control is a critical component that ensures the manageability, scalability, and traceability of infrastructure configurations. This section explores the importance of version control for infrastructure and best practices in this area.

Why Use Version Control for Infrastructure?

Version control systems (VCS), such as Git, play a pivotal role in managing infrastructure configurations. Here are some key reasons why version control is crucial:

1. **History and Auditing**: VCS allows you to maintain a historical record of all changes made to infrastructure configurations. This audit trail is invaluable for tracking modifications, identifying issues, and understanding the evolution of your infrastructure.
2. **Collaboration**: Version control enables collaboration among team members by providing a centralized repository where everyone can contribute changes,

comment on code, and review each other's work.

3. **Rollback and Recovery**: In case of errors or unexpected issues in infrastructure configurations, version control allows you to roll back to a previous known-good state, ensuring the reliability and stability of your environment.

4. **Parallel Development**: Different teams or individuals can work concurrently on different parts of the infrastructure code, and version control systems facilitate merging these changes seamlessly.

5. **Testing and Continuous Integration**: Integration with continuous integration (CI) and continuous deployment (CD) pipelines is simplified with version control. Automated tests can be triggered whenever changes are pushed to the repository, ensuring that new configurations are validated before deployment.

Best Practices for Version Controlling Infrastructure

To effectively version control infrastructure, consider the following best practices:

1. **Use Git**: Git is the most widely adopted version control system for infrastructure code. Ensure that your infrastructure code is stored in a Git repository.

2. **Repository Structure**: Organize your repository structure thoughtfully. Create directories and subdirectories to categorize configurations logically, making it easier to find and manage code.

3. **Branching Strategy**: Establish a branching strategy that suits your team's workflow. Common strategies include feature branching, Gitflow, or trunk-based development.

4. **Descriptive Commit Messages**: Write meaningful and descriptive commit messages that explain the purpose and

impact of each change.

5. **Pull Requests and Code Reviews**: Implement a process that involves creating pull requests for proposed changes and conducting code reviews. This ensures that changes are reviewed, tested, and validated before merging.

6. **Tagging Releases**: Use tags to mark significant releases or versions of your infrastructure code. This makes it easy to reference specific versions in your deployment pipeline.

7. **Automate Tests**: Integrate automated testing into your version control process. This includes unit tests, integration tests, and validation tests for infrastructure configurations.

Examples of Version Control in Infrastructure as Code

1. **Terraform with Git**: Terraform configurations can be version controlled using Git repositories. Each Terraform module or project can have its own Git repository, making it easy to manage and collaborate on infrastructure code.

2. **Ansible Playbooks**: Ansible playbooks for configuration management can be stored in Git repositories. Teams can create branches for different environments or projects and merge changes as needed.

3. **Docker Compose**: Docker Compose YAML files used to define multi-container applications can be version controlled with Git. Changes to the composition of containers can be tracked and managed via Git commits.

In conclusion, version control is an indispensable aspect of managing infrastructure as code. By adhering to best practices and leveraging version control systems like Git, organizations can ensure the reliability, stability, and traceability of their infrastructure

configurations while fostering collaboration and automation in the
DevOps pipeline.

6.5 Best Practices for Implementing IaC

Implementing Infrastructure as Code (IaC) involves more than just
writing code; it requires following best practices to ensure efficiency,
scalability, and maintainability of your infrastructure. In this section,
we'll explore key best practices for effectively implementing IaC.

1. Modularization and Reusability

Modularization is a fundamental concept in IaC. Break down your
infrastructure code into reusable modules, each responsible for a
specific component or functionality. This approach promotes code
reusability, simplifies maintenance, and allows you to compose
complex infrastructures from smaller, well-tested building blocks.

```
module "web_server" {

source = "./modules/web_server"

// Configuration parameters

}

module "database" {

source = "./modules/database"

// Configuration parameters

}
```

2. Parameterization

Parameterize your IaC code to make it flexible and adaptable to different environments. Use variables to define configuration values, allowing you to customize deployments for development, staging, and production environments easily.

```
variable "environment" {

description = "Deployment environment"

default = "dev"

}

resource "aws_instance" "web_server" {

ami = var.environment == "dev" ? "ami-dev" : "ami-prod"

instance_type = "t2.micro"

}
```

3. Version Control

Store your IaC code in a version control system (VCS), such as Git. This ensures version tracking, collaboration, and rollback capabilities. Create meaningful commit messages and use branching strategies that suit your team's workflow.

4. Testing

Implement automated testing for your IaC code. Tools like Terratest and Kitchen-Terraform enable you to write unit tests, integration tests, and validation tests for your infrastructure. Automated tests help catch errors early and ensure code reliability.

5. Documentation

Maintain clear and up-to-date documentation for your infrastructure code. Describe the purpose of modules, variables, and resources. Document the process for deploying and managing infrastructure, making it easier for team members to understand and use your code.

6. Continuous Integration and Continuous Deployment (CI/CD)

Integrate your IaC code into your CI/CD pipeline. Automate the deployment process, allowing changes to be tested and deployed automatically when code is pushed to the version control repository. This ensures consistency and reduces manual intervention.

7. Secret Management

Handle sensitive information, such as API keys and passwords, securely. Avoid hardcoding secrets in your code. Utilize secret management tools and vaults, like HashiCorp Vault or AWS Secrets Manager, to store and retrieve sensitive data.

8. Immutable Infrastructure

Adopt the concept of **immutable infrastructure**, where changes result in the creation of new instances rather than modifying existing ones. This approach simplifies rollback and ensures consistent and predictable deployments.

9. Monitoring and Logging

Implement monitoring and logging for your infrastructure. Use tools like Prometheus, Grafana, or CloudWatch to collect metrics and monitor resource health. Centralized logging solutions like Elasticsearch and Logstash can help you analyze logs effectively.

10. Compliance and Security

Adhere to industry best practices for security and compliance. Regularly audit your infrastructure code for vulnerabilities and ensure compliance with relevant standards and regulations. Implement security scanning tools and practices to identify and mitigate security risks.

11. Peer Review and Collaboration

Encourage peer review of IaC code changes. Collaborate with team members to ensure code quality and adherence to best practices. Code reviews help catch issues, share knowledge, and maintain code consistency.

12. Scalability and Performance

Design your infrastructure code with scalability and performance in mind. Consider horizontal scaling, load balancing, and auto-scaling capabilities to handle increased workloads gracefully.

Incorporating these best practices into your Infrastructure as Code implementation helps you build robust, reliable, and maintainable infrastructure while streamlining your DevOps processes. IaC, when done right, can significantly enhance your organization's agility and efficiency in managing and scaling infrastructure.

Chapter 7: Monitoring and Feedback Loops

7.1 Real-Time Monitoring and Alerting Systems

Real-time monitoring and alerting systems are essential components of a robust DevOps environment. They provide visibility into the health, performance, and availability of your applications and infrastructure, enabling proactive responses to issues and continuous improvement of your DevOps processes.

The Importance of Real-Time Monitoring

Real-time monitoring serves several critical purposes within a DevOps workflow:

1. **Early Issue Detection**: Monitoring systems continuously collect data on system performance and behavior. By analyzing this data in real-time, you can detect issues and anomalies as soon as they occur, often before they impact users or operations.

2. **Improved Incident Response**: When issues are detected in real-time, your team can respond quickly and effectively. Alerting mechanisms notify the relevant personnel or automation systems, allowing for rapid incident resolution and minimizing downtime.

3. **Performance Optimization**: Real-time monitoring provides insights into system performance trends. By identifying bottlenecks, resource constraints, or other performance issues early, you can proactively optimize your infrastructure and applications.

4. **Capacity Planning**: Monitoring helps you track resource utilization over time. This data is valuable for capacity planning and ensuring that your infrastructure can handle increasing workloads without performance degradation.

Components of Real-Time Monitoring

A typical real-time monitoring and alerting system consists of the following components:

1. **Data Collectors**: These agents or services collect data from various sources, such as servers, applications, and network devices. Common data types include performance metrics, log files, and event logs.

2. **Data Aggregators**: Data collected from multiple sources is aggregated and processed by centralized systems or services. This consolidation makes it easier to analyze and visualize the information.

3. **Alerting Rules**: Alerting rules define conditions that trigger alerts. For example, you might set a rule to generate an alert when CPU usage exceeds a certain threshold or when a specific error message appears in a log file.

4. **Alerting Mechanisms**: Alerts can be delivered through various channels, such as email, SMS, chat platforms, or integration with incident management tools like PagerDuty or OpsGenie. Alerting mechanisms ensure that the right people are notified promptly.

5. **Dashboards and Visualization**: Real-time monitoring often includes dashboards and visualization tools that display key performance metrics and trends. These visualizations provide at-a-glance insights into system health.

6. **Historical Data Storage**: Monitoring systems typically

store historical data for analysis, trending, and reporting. This data helps identify long-term trends and allows for post-incident analysis.

Common Monitoring Use Cases

Real-time monitoring and alerting systems can be applied to various use cases in a DevOps environment:

1. **Application Monitoring**: Monitor application performance, response times, error rates, and user experience to ensure optimal application delivery.
2. **Infrastructure Monitoring**: Track server health, resource utilization, and network performance to detect issues and plan for capacity upgrades.
3. **Security Monitoring**: Detect security threats and breaches by monitoring access logs, firewall logs, and system activity for suspicious behavior.
4. **Availability Monitoring**: Ensure that critical services and applications are available and responsive. Receive alerts when downtime or service disruptions occur.
5. **Performance Monitoring**: Continuously assess system performance and identify opportunities for optimization, whether it's improving database queries or optimizing web page load times.
6. **Compliance Monitoring**: Ensure compliance with industry regulations and internal policies by monitoring configurations and access controls.

Real-Time Monitoring Tools

A variety of real-time monitoring tools and solutions are available to DevOps teams, including open-source and commercial options. Some popular choices include:

- **Prometheus**: An open-source monitoring and alerting toolkit designed for reliability and scalability, commonly used with Grafana for visualization.

- **Nagios**: A widely used open-source monitoring system that can monitor hosts, services, and network devices.

- **ELK Stack (Elasticsearch, Logstash, Kibana)**: A combination of open-source tools used for log management, data analysis, and visualization.

- **Datadog**: A cloud-based monitoring and analytics platform that offers comprehensive monitoring solutions for cloud infrastructure, applications, and services.

- **New Relic**: A performance monitoring tool that provides insights into application performance and customer experience.

Implementing Real-Time Monitoring

To implement real-time monitoring effectively, follow these steps:

1. **Identify Key Metrics**: Determine which metrics and indicators are critical for your systems and applications. These will vary depending on your use case and objectives.
2. **Select Monitoring Tools**: Choose appropriate monitoring tools based on your infrastructure and requirements. Consider factors like scalability, integration capabilities,

and cost.

3. **Define Alerting Rules**: Establish alerting rules that specify when alerts should be triggered. Ensure that alerts are actionable and not prone to false positives.

4. **Implement Data Collectors**: Set up data collectors on relevant components of your infrastructure and applications. Configure these collectors to send data to your monitoring system.

5. **Create Dashboards**: Build dashboards and visualizations to display important metrics and trends. Dashboards provide a clear overview of system health.

6. **Set Up Alerting**: Configure alerting mechanisms to notify your team or automated systems when critical issues arise.

7. **Regularly Review and Optimize**: Continuously review your monitoring setup, adjust alerting rules as needed, and optimize system performance based on insights gained through monitoring.

In conclusion, real-time monitoring and alerting systems are integral to a successful DevOps practice. They enable proactive issue detection, rapid incident response, and ongoing performance optimization. By implementing these systems effectively and leveraging the right tools, DevOps teams can ensure the reliability and availability of their applications and infrastructure.

7.2 Implementing Effective Feedback Loops

Feedback loops are a fundamental component of the DevOps philosophy. They provide a mechanism for collecting information from various stages of the development and deployment process and using that information to drive continuous improvement. Effective feedback loops help teams identify issues, make informed decisions, and optimize their workflows.

The Importance of Feedback Loops

In the context of DevOps, feedback loops serve several critical purposes:

1. **Issue Detection**: Feedback loops allow teams to quickly detect and respond to issues and defects in both code and infrastructure. Early detection reduces the cost and impact of defects.
2. **Performance Monitoring**: Continuous feedback provides insights into system performance and behavior, helping teams optimize resource allocation and improve overall system performance.
3. **Quality Assurance**: Feedback loops enable automated testing and validation of code changes, ensuring that new features and updates meet quality standards.
4. **Risk Mitigation**: By identifying and addressing risks early in the development process, teams can reduce the likelihood of costly failures in production.
5. **Decision Support**: Feedback loops provide data-driven insights that support informed decision-making, whether it's choosing the best deployment strategy or prioritizing backlog items.

Types of Feedback Loops

DevOps encompasses various types of feedback loops, each serving a specific purpose:

1. **Development Feedback Loop**: This loop focuses on the development phase, providing developers with rapid

feedback on code changes. Continuous integration and automated testing are key components of this loop.

2. **Testing Feedback Loop**: Testing teams use this loop to validate code changes against predefined test cases. Automated testing tools and frameworks are often employed to speed up this process.

3. **Deployment Feedback Loop**: After code is deployed to production or staging environments, this loop monitors the application's behavior and performance. Real-time monitoring and alerting systems play a crucial role in this feedback loop.

4. **Operational Feedback Loop**: Operations teams use this loop to provide feedback on infrastructure performance, resource utilization, and system availability. Insights from this loop inform infrastructure scaling and optimization efforts.

5. **Customer Feedback Loop**: Gathering feedback directly from customers is essential for understanding their needs and improving user experience. Customer feedback can drive feature enhancements and bug fixes.

Implementing Effective Feedback Loops

To implement effective feedback loops in a DevOps environment, consider the following best practices:

1. **Automate Testing**: Automation is key to fast and reliable feedback. Implement automated testing processes at every stage of development and deployment, including unit tests, integration tests, and end-to-end tests.

2. **Continuous Integration (CI)**: Use CI pipelines to build, test, and validate code changes automatically whenever new code is pushed to version control. CI ensures that

feedback is immediate and consistent.

3. **Monitoring and Alerting**: Set up real-time monitoring and alerting systems to detect issues in production environments. Configure alerts to notify relevant teams or individuals when predefined thresholds are exceeded.

4. **Incident Response**: Establish clear incident response processes and procedures. When incidents occur, teams should follow well-defined workflows to investigate, mitigate, and resolve issues promptly.

5. **Feedback Channels**: Create channels for collecting feedback from all stakeholders, including developers, testers, operations teams, and customers. Use collaboration tools and communication platforms to facilitate feedback sharing.

6. **Metrics and Key Performance Indicators (KPIs)**: Define relevant metrics and KPIs to measure the effectiveness of feedback loops. Regularly analyze these metrics to identify areas for improvement.

7. **Continuous Improvement**: Encourage a culture of continuous improvement. Act on feedback and insights to refine processes, optimize workflows, and enhance overall performance.

8. **Feedback Loop Integration**: Ensure that feedback loops are integrated seamlessly into the DevOps toolchain. Feedback should flow naturally from one stage to another, promoting collaboration and transparency.

Tools for Feedback Loops

Several tools and technologies can assist in implementing effective feedback loops in DevOps:

- **Jenkins**: A popular CI/CD tool that automates the building, testing, and deployment of code changes.

- **Selenium**: An open-source framework for automating web browser testing.

- **Prometheus and Grafana**: Tools for monitoring and visualizing system metrics and performance data.

- **ELK Stack (Elasticsearch, Logstash, Kibana)**: A set of tools for centralized log management and analysis, which can aid in troubleshooting and feedback.

- **User Feedback Platforms**: Platforms like UserVoice and Zendesk provide mechanisms for gathering feedback directly from customers and users.

In summary, effective feedback loops are a cornerstone of successful DevOps practices. They enable teams to detect and address issues early, improve performance, and make data-driven decisions. By automating testing, implementing monitoring and alerting systems, and fostering a culture of continuous improvement, DevOps teams can optimize their feedback loops and enhance their overall development and deployment processes.

7.3 Using Analytics to Improve DevOps Processes

Analytics plays a crucial role in DevOps by providing valuable insights into the performance, efficiency, and quality of software development and delivery processes. By collecting and analyzing data from various stages of the DevOps pipeline, teams can identify bottlenecks, uncover optimization opportunities, and make data-driven decisions to continuously improve their processes. In this section, we'll explore how analytics can be leveraged to enhance DevOps practices.

The Role of Analytics in DevOps

Analytics in DevOps serves several key purposes:

1. **Performance Monitoring**: Analytics tools collect data on application performance, infrastructure utilization, and resource consumption. This information helps teams identify performance bottlenecks and optimize system resources.
2. **Quality Assurance**: Analyzing test results, code quality metrics, and defect data allows teams to assess the quality of their software and identify areas that require improvement.
3. **Root Cause Analysis**: When incidents or failures occur, analytics can assist in root cause analysis by correlating events and logs to pinpoint the underlying issues.
4. **Continuous Improvement**: Data-driven insights from analytics drive continuous improvement initiatives. Teams can use analytics to set benchmarks, track progress, and measure the impact of process changes.

Implementing Analytics in DevOps

To effectively implement analytics in a DevOps environment, consider the following steps:

1. **Define Metrics**: Start by defining the key performance indicators (KPIs) and metrics that are relevant to your DevOps processes. Metrics may include deployment frequency, lead time, change failure rate, and system

availability.

2. **Data Collection**: Implement mechanisms to collect data from various sources, such as CI/CD pipelines, monitoring tools, version control systems, and incident management platforms. Ensure that data is stored in a centralized repository for analysis.

3. **Data Analysis**: Utilize analytics tools and platforms to process and analyze the collected data. Common analytics tools in DevOps include Elasticsearch, Logstash, Kibana (ELK Stack), Prometheus, Grafana, and custom dashboards.

4. **Visualization**: Visualize the analyzed data using dashboards and reports. Visualization tools like Grafana and Kibana can provide real-time insights into the health and performance of your DevOps pipeline.

5. **Alerting**: Set up alerting mechanisms based on predefined thresholds and conditions. Alerts should notify relevant teams or individuals when deviations from expected behavior occur.

6. **Automation**: Implement automation to respond to certain conditions automatically. For example, automatically scaling resources based on workload or triggering automated incident responses.

7. **Continuous Monitoring**: Continuously monitor the effectiveness of your analytics and adjust metrics and alerts as needed. This ensures that analytics efforts remain aligned with evolving goals and objectives.

Metrics for DevOps Analytics

Here are some commonly used metrics in DevOps analytics:

1. **Deployment Frequency**: The frequency at which code

changes are deployed to production. High deployment frequency is a key DevOps goal.

2. **Lead Time**: The time it takes for a code change to go from commit to deployment. Short lead times are indicative of efficient processes.

3. **Change Failure Rate**: The percentage of code changes that result in failures or defects in production. Lower change failure rates indicate higher software quality.

4. **Mean Time to Recover (MTTR)**: The average time it takes to recover from incidents or failures. Reducing MTTR is essential for maintaining system availability.

5. **Resource Utilization**: Metrics related to resource consumption, such as CPU usage, memory utilization, and storage capacity.

6. **Defect Density**: The number of defects or issues identified per unit of code. Lower defect density indicates higher code quality.

7. **System Availability**: The percentage of time that a system is available and operational. High availability is critical for user satisfaction.

Tools for DevOps Analytics

Numerous tools and platforms can facilitate DevOps analytics:

- **Elasticsearch, Logstash, Kibana (ELK Stack)**: Used for log analysis, log management, and visualization.

- **Prometheus and Grafana**: A popular combination for monitoring and alerting, especially in Kubernetes environments.

- **Splunk**: A versatile platform for searching, analyzing, and visualizing machine-generated data.

- **New Relic**: Provides application performance monitoring (APM) and infrastructure monitoring capabilities.

- **Custom Analytics Dashboards**: Some organizations build custom dashboards using frameworks like D3.js or integrate analytics into their existing DevOps tools.

In conclusion, analytics is a powerful tool in DevOps, enabling teams to make informed decisions, optimize processes, and deliver higher-quality software. By defining relevant metrics, collecting and analyzing data, and leveraging appropriate analytics tools, organizations can gain deeper insights into their DevOps practices and continuously improve their software development and delivery pipelines.

7.4 Post-Deployment Monitoring Strategies

Post-deployment monitoring is a critical aspect of DevOps, focusing on the continuous assessment and optimization of applications and infrastructure after they are in production. This stage ensures that the deployed software operates efficiently, meets performance expectations, and remains stable. In this section, we will explore post-deployment monitoring strategies and best practices in DevOps.

The Importance of Post-Deployment Monitoring

Post-deployment monitoring serves several essential purposes:

1. **Issue Detection**: It helps identify performance

bottlenecks, errors, and issues that might not have been evident during testing.

2. **Performance Evaluation**: Teams can assess how the application performs under real-world conditions and make necessary adjustments for optimization.

3. **Resource Management**: Monitoring assists in resource allocation and optimization, ensuring that infrastructure resources are used efficiently.

4. **User Experience**: Monitoring helps gauge the end-user experience, ensuring that the application meets user expectations.

Key Post-Deployment Monitoring Strategies

1. **Real-Time Monitoring**: Implement real-time monitoring tools and dashboards to track system health, application performance, and user interactions in real time. Tools like Prometheus and Grafana can be instrumental in this regard.

2. **Logs and Event Data**: Collect and analyze logs and event data generated by the application and infrastructure components. Centralized log management solutions like ELK Stack (Elasticsearch, Logstash, Kibana) are commonly used for this purpose.

3. **Alerting and Notification**: Set up alerting mechanisms to proactively detect and respond to anomalies, errors, and performance issues. Alerts should be triggered based on predefined thresholds and conditions.

4. **Incident Response**: Develop incident response plans to address critical issues promptly. Establish procedures for escalating incidents, coordinating responses, and performing post-incident reviews.

5. **Performance Metrics**: Monitor key performance

indicators (KPIs) such as response time, latency, throughput, and error rates. Use these metrics to identify areas for improvement.

6. **Resource Utilization**: Keep an eye on resource utilization metrics such as CPU, memory, and disk usage. Adjust resource allocation as needed to optimize performance and cost-efficiency.

7. **User Experience Monitoring**: Measure and track user experience metrics, including page load times, error rates, and user interactions. This provides insights into how users perceive the application's performance.

8. **Security Monitoring**: Integrate security monitoring into your post-deployment strategy. Continuously scan for vulnerabilities, monitor access logs, and respond to security incidents promptly.

Best Practices for Post-Deployment Monitoring

To ensure effective post-deployment monitoring, consider the following best practices:

1. **Automate Monitoring**: Implement automated monitoring processes and tools to reduce manual effort and ensure continuous coverage.

2. **Establish Baselines**: Create baseline performance and resource utilization metrics to compare against when issues arise. This helps in quickly identifying deviations from expected behavior.

3. **Collaborative Approach**: Encourage collaboration between development, operations, and security teams to collectively address issues and improvements.

4. **Scalability**: Ensure that monitoring solutions are scalable to accommodate growing workloads and infrastructure.

5. **Regular Reviews**: Conduct regular reviews of post-deployment monitoring data to identify trends, patterns, and recurring issues.

6. **Feedback Loop**: Establish a feedback loop from post-deployment monitoring to development and testing stages. Use insights gained to inform future development and deployment decisions.

7. **Compliance Monitoring**: Incorporate compliance monitoring to ensure that applications adhere to regulatory and security standards.

8. **Documentation**: Document post-deployment monitoring processes, alerting rules, and incident response procedures for reference and training purposes.

Tools for Post-Deployment Monitoring

Several tools and technologies are commonly used for post-deployment monitoring in DevOps, including:

- **Prometheus and Grafana**: Popular for real-time monitoring and alerting.

- **ELK Stack (Elasticsearch, Logstash, Kibana)**: Useful for centralized log management and analysis.

- **New Relic and AppDynamics**: Application performance monitoring (APM) solutions.

- **Nagios**: Known for its robust alerting and monitoring capabilities.

- **Splunk**: A versatile platform for analyzing machine-generated data, including logs and events.

- **Security Tools**: Security-focused tools like Nessus and Security Information and Event Management (SIEM) systems for security monitoring.

In summary, post-deployment monitoring is a crucial phase in the DevOps lifecycle, ensuring that applications and infrastructure operate efficiently and meet user expectations. By implementing real-time monitoring, analyzing logs and events, setting up alerting mechanisms, and following best practices, DevOps teams can proactively address issues, optimize performance, and deliver a better user experience.

7.5 Continuous Improvement Through Feedback

Continuous improvement is a core principle in DevOps, and feedback loops play a pivotal role in achieving this goal. In this section, we will delve into the concept of continuous improvement through feedback and how it contributes to the success of DevOps practices.

The Significance of Feedback Loops

Feedback loops in DevOps are mechanisms for collecting information about the performance, quality, and efficiency of software development and deployment processes. These loops provide insights that help teams make informed decisions, optimize workflows, and enhance overall efficiency.

Key aspects of feedback loops include:

1. **Speed**: Feedback loops are designed to provide information quickly, allowing teams to respond to issues or improvements promptly.

2. **Visibility**: They offer visibility into various stages of the development and deployment pipeline, including code changes, testing, and production.
3. **Learning**: Feedback loops facilitate a culture of learning and adaptation, enabling teams to continuously evolve and improve their practices.

Types of Feedback Loops in DevOps

1. **Automated Testing**: Continuous integration (CI) pipelines often include automated testing stages. Feedback from these tests highlights code quality, identifies bugs, and verifies that new changes meet acceptance criteria.
2. **User Feedback**: Direct feedback from end-users is invaluable. Gathering user feedback through surveys, user support channels, and monitoring user behavior helps prioritize enhancements and bug fixes.
3. **Monitoring and Alerting**: Real-time monitoring and alerting systems provide feedback on application and infrastructure health. Alerts notify teams of issues or performance anomalies, allowing rapid response.
4. **Code Review**: Code review processes involve peer reviews of code changes. Feedback from reviewers helps maintain code quality, adherence to coding standards, and knowledge sharing.
5. **Post-Incident Reviews**: After resolving incidents, conducting post-incident reviews (PIRs) provides feedback on what went wrong, why it happened, and how to prevent similar incidents in the future.

Implementing Effective Feedback Loops

To maximize the benefits of feedback loops in DevOps, consider the following strategies:

1. **Automation**: Automate the collection and analysis of feedback whenever possible. Automated testing, monitoring, and alerting tools streamline the process.
2. **Clear Objectives**: Define clear objectives and key performance indicators (KPIs) for feedback loops. What do you want to measure, and how will you interpret the data?
3. **Closed-Loop Feedback**: Ensure that feedback leads to action. Identify improvement opportunities and create action items based on feedback.
4. **Collaboration**: Encourage collaboration between development, operations, and other stakeholders to collectively interpret feedback and make informed decisions.
5. **Continuous Monitoring**: Maintain continuous monitoring of feedback loops to detect and address issues early, preventing them from escalating.
6. **Feedback Culture**: Foster a culture that values feedback, where team members feel safe providing input and suggesting improvements.
7. **Data-Driven Decision-Making**: Base decisions on data and evidence gathered from feedback loops rather than assumptions or gut feelings.

Benefits of Continuous Improvement Through Feedback

Effective feedback loops in DevOps yield several benefits:

1. **Faster Issue Resolution**: Rapidly identify and address issues, reducing downtime and improving user satisfaction.

2. **Higher Quality Software**: Continuous feedback results in higher code quality and fewer defects, leading to more stable applications.

3. **Optimized Workflows**: Identify bottlenecks and inefficiencies in processes and workflows, leading to process optimization.

4. **Improved Collaboration**: Cross-functional teams collaborate more effectively when armed with relevant feedback.

5. **Informed Decision-Making**: Data-driven decision-making leads to more informed choices, reducing risks and enhancing outcomes.

6. **Adaptability**: Teams become more adaptable and responsive to changing requirements and challenges.

In conclusion, continuous improvement through feedback loops is a fundamental principle in DevOps, driving enhanced software quality, optimized processes, and a culture of learning and collaboration. Embracing feedback as a valuable asset can lead to more efficient and effective DevOps practices.

Chapter 8: Security in DevOps (DevSecOps)

8.1 Integrating Security into the DevOps Lifecycle

In the realm of modern software development, security is not an afterthought but an integral part of the process. DevOps, with its focus on automation, collaboration, and continuous delivery, provides the perfect platform for integrating security practices seamlessly into the software development lifecycle. This chapter explores the concept of DevSecOps, highlighting its importance and best practices for effectively integrating security into DevOps processes.

The Shift Left Approach

One of the foundational principles of DevSecOps is the "Shift Left" approach. Traditionally, security assessments and testing were performed late in the software development cycle, often just before deployment. In contrast, the Shift Left approach emphasizes moving security practices to the earliest stages of development.

By embedding security from the beginning, developers can identify and address security vulnerabilities and issues proactively, saving time and resources in the long run. This approach aligns perfectly with the DevOps principle of automating everything, as security checks can be automated and integrated into the CI/CD pipeline.

Key Components of DevSecOps

To effectively integrate security into DevOps, consider the following key components:

1. Security as Code

Treat security policies, controls, and configurations as code. This means defining security requirements in code and version-controlling them. Tools like Infrastructure as Code (IaC) and Policy as Code (PaC) help automate and manage security configurations.

2. Automated Security Testing

Implement automated security testing throughout the development pipeline. This includes static analysis (SAST), dynamic analysis (DAST), and interactive analysis (IAST) tools that scan code and applications for vulnerabilities.

3. Continuous Compliance

Enforce compliance with security standards and regulations using automation. Tools can continuously monitor and report on compliance status, making it easier to identify and address violations.

4. Threat Modeling

Incorporate threat modeling into the design phase to identify potential security threats and vulnerabilities. Address these threats early in the development process.

5. Security Training and Awareness

Provide security training and awareness programs for development and operations teams. Knowledgeable teams are better equipped to make security-conscious decisions.

6. Access Control and Identity Management

Implement strong access controls and identity management practices. Ensure that only authorized individuals have access to critical systems and data.

7. Incident Response Planning

Develop and maintain an incident response plan. Ensure that teams are prepared to respond effectively to security incidents and breaches.

DevSecOps Benefits

Integrating security into DevOps practices offers several advantages:

1. **Early Issue Identification**: Security vulnerabilities are identified and addressed at an early stage, reducing the cost and effort of remediation.
2. **Consistency**: Security policies are consistently applied across environments, reducing the risk of misconfigurations.
3. **Compliance**: Automated compliance checks help maintain adherence to regulatory requirements.
4. **Improved Collaboration**: Collaboration between security, development, and operations teams fosters a culture of shared responsibility for security.
5. **Faster Delivery**: Security automation speeds up the release process by eliminating manual security checks.
6. **Reduced Risk**: Proactive security practices reduce the risk of data breaches and security incidents.

Incorporating security into DevOps practices through the DevSecOps approach is not only a best practice but also a necessity in today's cybersecurity landscape. It ensures that security is not a hindrance to development but an enabler for delivering secure and reliable software.

8.2 Tools and Practices for DevSecOps

DevSecOps relies on a combination of tools and practices to integrate security seamlessly into the DevOps pipeline. These tools and practices help organizations identify vulnerabilities, enforce security policies, and respond to security incidents effectively. In this section, we will explore some essential tools and practices that facilitate the DevSecOps approach.

Security Scanning Tools

One of the foundational elements of DevSecOps is the use of security scanning tools that automatically analyze code, applications, and infrastructure for vulnerabilities. These tools help identify issues early in the development process. Here are some common types of security scanning tools:

1. **Static Application Security Testing (SAST)**: SAST tools analyze source code or binary code to identify vulnerabilities and security issues without executing the code. Examples include Checkmarx and SonarQube.
2. **Dynamic Application Security Testing (DAST)**: DAST tools assess running applications from the outside, simulating attacks to identify vulnerabilities that can be exploited. Examples include OWASP ZAP and Burp Suite.
3. **Container Scanning**: Container security tools like Clair and Trivy scan container images for known vulnerabilities

and provide insights into potential risks.

4. **Infrastructure as Code (IaC) Scanning**: Tools like Terraform and AWS Config can scan infrastructure code to identify security misconfigurations and compliance violations.

Security Orchestration and Automation

Automation plays a crucial role in DevSecOps, enabling security checks and responses to occur automatically as part of the CI/CD pipeline. Here are some key automation practices and tools:

1. **Security Policies as Code**: Define security policies and configurations as code using tools like HashiCorp Sentinel or Open Policy Agent (OPA). This allows automated checks for compliance with security policies.

2. **CI/CD Pipeline Integration**: Integrate security checks into your CI/CD pipeline using tools such as Jenkins, Travis CI, or GitLab CI/CD. Automated security scans should be part of the pipeline stages.

3. **Security Orchestration**: Use orchestration tools like Ansible or Puppet to automate security-related tasks, such as applying patches or responding to security incidents.

4. **Incident Response Automation**: Implement incident response automation with tools like Phantom or Demisto. These tools help orchestrate incident response actions when security incidents occur.

Infrastructure Security as Code (IaC)

Infrastructure as Code (IaC) is a DevSecOps practice that treats infrastructure provisioning and configuration as code. It enables consistent and automated infrastructure deployments while maintaining security. Key aspects of IaC in DevSecOps include:

1. **Automated Provisioning**: Use IaC tools like Terraform, AWS CloudFormation, or Azure Resource Manager templates to automate the provisioning of infrastructure resources securely.
2. **Security Baseline Templates**: Create IaC templates that define security baselines and best practices for infrastructure components. This ensures that security is built into the infrastructure.
3. **Continuous Scanning**: Implement continuous scanning of IaC templates for security vulnerabilities and misconfigurations using tools like Checkov or Terrascan.

Security Training and Awareness

DevSecOps is not just about tools; it also involves building a security-aware culture within the organization. Security training and awareness programs for development and operations teams are essential. These programs should cover topics such as secure coding practices, threat modeling, and incident response procedures.

Threat Modeling

Threat modeling is a practice that involves identifying and mitigating security threats and vulnerabilities during the design phase of a project. It helps teams understand potential risks and make informed security decisions. Tools like Microsoft Threat Modeling Tool or OWASP Threat Dragon can assist in the threat modeling process.

Continuous Monitoring and Logging

Continuous monitoring of applications and infrastructure is critical for identifying security incidents and anomalies. Security Information and Event Management (SIEM) tools like Splunk or ELK Stack can be used for real-time monitoring and log analysis. Implementing centralized logging and monitoring solutions helps detect security issues promptly.

In summary, DevSecOps relies on a combination of security scanning tools, automation, Infrastructure as Code, security training, threat modeling, and continuous monitoring to integrate security into the DevOps pipeline effectively. These tools and practices help organizations proactively address security concerns and deliver secure software at a faster pace.

8.3 Handling Vulnerabilities and Patches

In the realm of DevSecOps, addressing vulnerabilities and applying patches promptly is crucial to maintaining a secure and resilient software ecosystem. Vulnerabilities can be introduced through various stages of the development lifecycle, and detecting and remedying them in a timely manner is essential to minimize potential security risks. This section discusses practices and strategies for effectively handling vulnerabilities and patches within a DevSecOps environment.

Vulnerability Assessment

DevSecOps teams should regularly perform vulnerability assessments to identify security weaknesses in their applications and infrastructure. These assessments involve the use of automated scanning tools, penetration testing, and code analysis to uncover vulnerabilities.

Automated Scanning Tools

- Utilize automated scanning tools like Nessus, Qualys, or OpenVAS to scan your infrastructure and applications for known vulnerabilities.

- Incorporate container security scanning tools such as Clair or Trivy into your CI/CD pipeline to detect vulnerabilities in container images before deployment.

- Implement static application security testing (SAST) tools like Checkmarx or SonarQube to identify security flaws in the source code.

Penetration Testing

- Conduct regular penetration testing to simulate real-world attacks and identify vulnerabilities that automated tools might miss.

- Engage third-party security experts or red teams to assess your system's security posture from an external perspective.

Vulnerability Prioritization

Not all vulnerabilities are created equal, and it's essential to prioritize and address them based on their severity and potential impact on your system. DevSecOps teams can follow these practices:

- **CVSS Scoring**: Use the Common Vulnerability Scoring System (CVSS) to assign scores to vulnerabilities, helping you prioritize them based on factors like exploitability, impact, and complexity.

- **Risk Assessment:** Perform risk assessments to understand the business impact of vulnerabilities and prioritize those that pose the most significant risk.

- **Vulnerability Intelligence:** Stay informed about emerging threats and vulnerabilities by subscribing to security feeds and mailing lists.

Patch Management

Once vulnerabilities are identified and prioritized, effective patch management is essential to mitigate these risks. The following practices can aid in efficient patch management:

- **Automated Patching:** Implement automated patch management systems to apply security patches promptly. Tools like Ansible, Puppet, or Chef can be valuable in automating this process.

- **Patch Testing:** Before deploying patches to production, test them in a staging environment to ensure they do not introduce new issues.

- **Rollback Plan:** Develop a rollback plan in case a patch causes unforeseen problems. Being prepared for potential issues minimizes downtime and disruptions.

- **Continuous Monitoring:** Continuously monitor your systems for vulnerabilities, even after patching. Some vulnerabilities may require ongoing mitigation strategies.

Vulnerability Response

In a DevSecOps environment, it's essential to have a well-defined vulnerability response process in place. This includes clear communication channels and workflows for addressing vulnerabilities:

- **Incident Response Plan**: Develop an incident response plan that outlines how your organization will respond to security incidents, including vulnerabilities.

- **Communication Channels**: Establish effective communication channels within your team and with relevant stakeholders to report, discuss, and coordinate the resolution of vulnerabilities.

- **Security Documentation**: Maintain documentation of vulnerabilities, patches applied, and lessons learned for future reference and improvement.

Continuous Improvement

DevSecOps is a continuous journey of improvement. After addressing vulnerabilities, it's essential to learn from the experience and enhance your security practices:

- **Post-Incident Analysis**: Conduct post-incident analysis to understand the root causes of vulnerabilities and identify areas for improvement.

- **Feedback Loops**: Establish feedback loops between security, development, and operations teams to share knowledge and improve security awareness.

- **Training and Awareness:** Provide ongoing training and awareness programs to keep your teams updated on the latest security threats and best practices.

In conclusion, handling vulnerabilities and patches is a critical aspect of DevSecOps, ensuring the security and stability of your software systems. By following practices such as vulnerability assessment, prioritization, effective patch management, and continuous improvement, DevSecOps teams can proactively manage security risks and maintain a resilient software ecosystem.

8.4 Compliance and Security Standards

In the world of DevSecOps, compliance with industry-specific and regulatory security standards is a critical concern. Organizations must adhere to these standards to ensure the security and privacy of their data, protect their reputation, and avoid legal consequences. This section delves into the importance of compliance and the strategies for incorporating security standards into DevSecOps practices.

The Significance of Compliance

Compliance with security standards is essential for several reasons:

1. **Legal Obligations:** Many industries are subject to specific regulations and legal requirements governing data protection and security. Failing to comply can result in hefty fines and legal penalties.
2. **Data Protection:** Compliance standards often include guidelines for safeguarding sensitive data, such as customer information and financial records. Ensuring compliance is crucial for protecting this data from breaches.

3. **Customer Trust**: Adhering to recognized security standards can enhance customer trust. It demonstrates a commitment to data security and privacy, which can be a competitive advantage.

4. **Risk Mitigation**: Compliance standards often provide best practices for mitigating security risks. By following these practices, organizations can reduce their vulnerability to threats and attacks.

Incorporating Compliance into DevSecOps

Integrating compliance into DevSecOps practices requires a holistic approach that considers both development processes and security measures:

1. **Mapping Requirements**: Start by identifying the specific compliance requirements that apply to your organization and industry. This includes regulations like GDPR, HIPAA, PCI DSS, or industry-specific standards.

2. **Automated Testing**: Implement automated security testing and scanning tools that check code and infrastructure for compliance violations. These tools can identify issues early in the development process.

3. **Continuous Monitoring**: Continuously monitor your infrastructure and applications to detect compliance violations in real-time. Utilize log analysis, intrusion detection systems, and security information and event management (SIEM) solutions.

4. **Security Policies as Code**: Define security policies as code by codifying compliance rules and checks into your infrastructure-as-code (IaC) templates. This ensures that security and compliance are maintained as part of the deployment process.

5. **Auditing and Reporting**: Regularly conduct audits and generate compliance reports. These reports provide evidence of compliance for regulatory authorities and stakeholders.

6. **Security Champions**: Appoint security champions within your DevSecOps teams who are responsible for advocating and enforcing compliance standards. They bridge the gap between security and development.

7. **Education and Training**: Educate your development and operations teams about compliance requirements and best practices. Ensure that they understand the importance of compliance and their role in maintaining it.

8. **Documentation**: Maintain clear and organized documentation of compliance-related processes, checks, and audits. This documentation is essential for regulatory audits and demonstrating adherence to standards.

Common Compliance Standards

There are several well-known compliance standards that organizations often need to adhere to:

- **GDPR (General Data Protection Regulation)**: Protects the privacy and personal data of European Union citizens. It applies to any organization that processes EU citizen data.

- **HIPAA (Health Insurance Portability and Accountability Act)**: Applies to healthcare organizations and addresses the security and privacy of patient information.

- **PCI DSS (Payment Card Industry Data Security Standard)**: Mandatory for organizations that handle credit card transactions and data.

- **ISO 27001**: A globally recognized standard for information security management systems (ISMS).

- **NIST Cybersecurity Framework**: Developed by the National Institute of Standards and Technology (NIST) to improve cybersecurity across industries.

In summary, compliance and security standards are paramount in DevSecOps, ensuring that organizations meet legal requirements, protect sensitive data, and maintain customer trust. By integrating compliance into the DevSecOps pipeline through automated testing, continuous monitoring, and policy enforcement, organizations can achieve a higher level of security and regulatory adherence.

8.5 Building a Culture of Security Awareness

In the DevSecOps paradigm, building a culture of security awareness is paramount to ensuring that security is everyone's responsibility, not just the concern of a specialized security team. A security-aware culture involves educating and empowering all members of an organization to recognize and mitigate security risks. This section explores the significance of security awareness and offers strategies for fostering it within DevSecOps teams.

The Importance of Security Awareness

1. **Reducing Human Errors**: A significant number of security breaches result from human errors, such as clicking

on phishing emails or misconfiguring systems. Security
awareness programs aim to reduce these errors through
education and training.

2. **Early Detection**: Security-aware employees are more likely
to detect and report security incidents promptly. This can
lead to quicker response times and reduced damage in case
of a breach.

3. **Mitigating Insider Threats**: Insider threats, where
employees intentionally or unintentionally compromise
security, can be mitigated through awareness programs that
emphasize the consequences of such actions.

4. **Regulatory Compliance**: Many regulatory standards
require organizations to have security awareness programs
in place. Compliance with these standards is crucial to
avoid penalties.

Strategies for Building Security Awareness

1. **Training Programs**: Develop comprehensive training
programs that cover security best practices, the
organization's security policies, and specific threat
scenarios. Training should be tailored to different roles
within the organization.

2. **Phishing Simulations**: Conduct regular phishing
simulations to test employees' ability to recognize and
respond to phishing emails. Provide feedback and
additional training to those who fall for simulated attacks.

3. **Continuous Learning**: Security awareness is an ongoing
process. Encourage employees to stay updated on the latest
security threats and best practices through continuous
learning opportunities.

4. **Secure Coding Training**: If your organization develops
software, offer secure coding training to developers. Teach

them how to write code that is less susceptible to common vulnerabilities.

5. **Awareness Campaigns**: Run awareness campaigns that focus on specific security topics. These can include topics like password hygiene, social engineering, and data protection.

6. **Reward Systems**: Implement reward systems that recognize and incentivize employees for their contributions to security awareness and incident reporting.

7. **Security Champions**: Appoint security champions within different teams who serve as advocates for security practices and help disseminate security knowledge.

8. **Reporting Mechanisms**: Provide clear and easily accessible channels for employees to report security incidents or concerns anonymously, if necessary.

9. **Leadership Support**: Ensure that leadership actively supports and participates in security awareness initiatives. Their involvement sends a strong message about the importance of security.

Measuring Security Awareness

To gauge the effectiveness of security awareness programs, organizations can use metrics such as:

- **Phishing Simulation Results**: Track the percentage of employees who fall for phishing simulations and monitor improvements over time.

- **Incident Reporting**: Measure the number of security incidents reported by employees and the response time to address them.

- **Training Completion Rates:** Monitor the completion rates of security training programs and assess whether employees are engaging with the material.

- **Feedback and Surveys:** Collect feedback from employees through surveys to understand their perceptions of the security culture.

- **Reduction in Security Incidents:** Track the overall reduction in security incidents and breaches as a result of improved security awareness.

In conclusion, building a culture of security awareness is a fundamental aspect of DevSecOps. It empowers all members of an organization to contribute to security efforts and reduces the risk of security breaches. By implementing comprehensive training programs, continuous learning opportunities, and other awareness initiatives, organizations can create a security-conscious environment that protects sensitive data and mitigates threats effectively.

Chapter 9: Cloud Computing and DevOps

9.1 Leveraging Cloud Services for DevOps

Cloud computing has revolutionized the way organizations approach software development and operations. It offers a scalable, flexible, and cost-effective infrastructure that aligns well with DevOps practices. In this section, we will explore the integration of cloud services with DevOps and the benefits it brings to the development and deployment processes.

The Intersection of Cloud Computing and DevOps

1. **Scalability**: Cloud platforms like Amazon Web Services (AWS), Microsoft Azure, and Google Cloud provide the ability to scale resources up or down dynamically. DevOps teams can leverage this feature to meet changing demands efficiently.

2. **Automation**: Cloud services offer extensive automation capabilities, which align perfectly with the automation principles of DevOps. Infrastructure as Code (IaC) tools and serverless computing further automate infrastructure provisioning and application deployment.

3. **Elasticity**: Cloud resources can be easily configured to scale horizontally and vertically, allowing applications to handle sudden spikes in traffic without manual intervention.

4. **Cost Optimization**: DevOps teams can optimize costs by provisioning resources as needed and shutting them down during periods of inactivity. This pay-as-you-go model can lead to significant cost savings.

5. **Global Reach**: Cloud providers offer data centers and services in multiple regions globally. This allows DevOps teams to deploy applications closer to end-users for lower latency and improved performance.

DevOps Practices in the Cloud

1. **Continuous Integration and Deployment (CI/CD)**: Cloud platforms provide managed services for building CI/CD pipelines. DevOps teams can leverage these services to automate the testing and deployment of applications.

2. **Infrastructure as Code (IaC)**: Cloud environments support IaC tools like AWS CloudFormation, Azure Resource Manager templates, and Terraform. This enables infrastructure provisioning and management through code, enhancing reproducibility and scalability.

3. **Monitoring and Logging**: Cloud platforms offer robust monitoring and logging solutions. DevOps teams can use these tools to gain visibility into application performance and troubleshoot issues proactively.

4. **Security**: Cloud providers offer security services like Identity and Access Management (IAM), encryption, and security groups. DevOps teams can integrate these services into their security practices to ensure a secure environment.

Challenges in Cloud DevOps

While the integration of cloud computing and DevOps brings numerous advantages, it also presents some challenges:

1. **Complexity**: Managing cloud resources and configurations can become complex, especially in large-scale deployments.

Effective IaC practices and automation are essential to manage this complexity.

2. **Cost Management**: Cloud costs can escalate if not managed properly. DevOps teams need to continuously monitor and optimize resource usage to avoid unexpected expenses.

3. **Vendor Lock-In**: Depending on a specific cloud provider can lead to vendor lock-in. DevOps teams should consider multi-cloud strategies to mitigate this risk.

4. **Security Concerns**: While cloud providers offer robust security features, misconfigurations and security breaches are still possible. DevOps teams must prioritize security practices and regular audits.

5. **Compliance**: Organizations in regulated industries need to ensure that their cloud deployments comply with industry-specific regulations. This can add complexity to DevOps processes.

In summary, cloud computing and DevOps are highly complementary, offering the flexibility, scalability, and automation needed for modern software development and operations. DevOps teams should carefully plan and implement their cloud strategies, considering the benefits and challenges of cloud integration.

9.2 Cloud Infrastructure and DevOps Synergy

DevOps practices and cloud infrastructure have become inseparable components of modern software development and deployment. In this section, we'll delve into the synergy between cloud infrastructure and DevOps and how they enable organizations to achieve greater efficiency, agility, and scalability.

Cloud-Native Development

DevOps principles emphasize automation, collaboration, and continuous delivery, all of which align with the cloud-native approach to application development. Cloud-native applications are designed to run in cloud environments and take full advantage of cloud services. DevOps teams leverage cloud-native development to build and deploy applications more efficiently.

Key Synergies:

1. **On-Demand Resources**: Cloud platforms provide on-demand access to computing resources, storage, and networking. DevOps teams can dynamically provision and de-provision resources as needed, ensuring optimal resource utilization and cost savings.

2. **Infrastructure as Code (IaC)**: IaC tools like Terraform, AWS CloudFormation, and Azure Resource Manager enable the definition and provisioning of cloud resources through code. This aligns with the automation and version control principles of DevOps, allowing infrastructure to be managed as code.

3. **Scalability**: Cloud environments offer auto-scaling capabilities, enabling applications to scale horizontally or vertically in response to changing workloads. DevOps teams can configure auto-scaling to maintain performance and availability.

4. **Continuous Integration and Deployment (CI/CD)**: Cloud services provide integrated CI/CD pipelines that streamline code integration, testing, and deployment. DevOps practices are closely integrated with these cloud-native CI/CD pipelines, facilitating automated and rapid software releases.

5. **Managed Services**: Cloud providers offer managed services for databases, caching, messaging, and more. DevOps teams can leverage these services to offload operational tasks, focus on application development, and ensure high availability.

Best Practices:

1. **Align Cloud Strategy with DevOps Goals**: Define a clear cloud strategy that aligns with DevOps principles and goals. Consider factors like multi-cloud, hybrid cloud, and cloud-native development.
2. **Leverage Cloud-Native Services**: Embrace cloud-native services to simplify infrastructure management. Utilize managed services for databases, container orchestration, and serverless computing to reduce operational overhead.
3. **Implement Infrastructure as Code**: Use IaC to define, version, and provision cloud resources. This practice enhances reproducibility, automates resource management, and ensures consistency across environments.
4. **Monitor and Optimize Costs**: Continuously monitor cloud resource usage and costs. Implement cost optimization practices, such as rightsizing instances and shutting down unused resources to avoid unexpected expenses.
5. **Security and Compliance**: Prioritize security in cloud deployments. Implement security best practices, configure network access controls, and perform regular security audits. Ensure compliance with industry-specific regulations.
6. **Backup and Disaster Recovery**: Develop robust backup and disaster recovery plans specific to your cloud environment. Test these plans regularly to ensure data

integrity and availability.

Challenges:

1. **Complexity**: Managing cloud-native applications and infrastructure can introduce complexity. DevOps teams must invest in training and tools to effectively navigate this complexity.
2. **Cost Management**: While cloud offers cost advantages, improper resource allocation can lead to overruns. DevOps teams need to carefully manage and optimize cloud costs.
3. **Security**: Cloud security is a shared responsibility between the cloud provider and the customer. DevOps teams must implement security measures to protect applications and data.
4. **Data Management**: Handling data in the cloud, especially across different regions or providers, can be challenging. Robust data management strategies are essential for data integrity and compliance.

In conclusion, the synergy between cloud infrastructure and DevOps is a driving force behind the transformation of software development and deployment practices. Organizations that embrace cloud-native development and align it with DevOps principles can achieve greater agility, scalability, and efficiency in delivering high-quality software products to their users.

9.3 Scaling and Elasticity in Cloud Environments

Scaling and elasticity are fundamental concepts in cloud computing, and they play a crucial role in the context of DevOps. In this section, we will explore how DevOps teams leverage the scalability and elasticity offered by cloud environments to ensure optimal performance, resource utilization, and cost-efficiency.

Understanding Scaling

Scaling refers to the process of adjusting the capacity of an application or system to meet changing demands. It can be categorized into two main types:

1. **Vertical Scaling (Upward Scaling)**: Involves increasing the capacity of individual resources, such as adding more CPU or RAM to a virtual machine. Vertical scaling is often limited by the maximum capacity of a single resource.
2. **Horizontal Scaling (Outward Scaling)**: Involves adding more instances of a resource, such as replicating web servers or database nodes. Horizontal scaling is highly scalable and can handle a large number of requests.

Elasticity in Cloud Environments

Elasticity is a characteristic of cloud computing that enables resources to automatically scale up or down based on real-time demand. DevOps teams can leverage elasticity to ensure that applications are responsive and cost-effective.

Key aspects of elasticity in cloud environments include:

1. **Auto-Scaling**: Cloud providers offer auto-scaling features that allow resources to automatically adjust based on predefined policies or metrics. For example, when CPU utilization exceeds a certain threshold, additional instances can be launched to handle the load.
2. **Load Balancing**: Load balancers distribute incoming traffic across multiple instances, ensuring even distribution

and high availability. This is essential for horizontally
scaled applications.

3. **Dynamic Resource Provisioning**: DevOps teams can use
Infrastructure as Code (IaC) and cloud orchestration tools
to dynamically provision resources as needed. This ensures
that infrastructure can scale with the application.

Benefits of Scaling and Elasticity in DevOps

DevOps practices are closely intertwined with scaling and elasticity
in cloud environments, offering several advantages:

1. **Improved Performance**: Scalability allows applications to
maintain optimal performance, even during traffic spikes
or high load periods.

2. **Cost Optimization**: With elasticity, resources are
provisioned as needed, reducing unnecessary costs
associated with overprovisioning. Conversely, resources
can be scaled down during low-demand periods to save on
expenses.

3. **High Availability**: Horizontal scaling and load balancing
enhance the availability of applications by distributing
traffic across multiple instances. Failures in individual
resources have minimal impact.

4. **Flexibility and Agility**: DevOps teams can quickly adapt
to changing requirements, whether it's handling increased
user demand or rolling out new features. This agility is
crucial in fast-paced development environments.

Implementing Scaling and Elasticity in DevOps

To effectively implement scaling and elasticity in DevOps, consider
the following best practices:

1. **Define Scaling Policies**: Clearly define scaling policies based on key performance metrics, such as CPU utilization, memory usage, or network traffic. These policies should trigger automatic scaling actions.

2. **Automate Resource Provisioning**: Use Infrastructure as Code (IaC) tools to automate the provisioning of resources. Define templates that specify the desired infrastructure configuration, and use automation scripts to deploy and scale resources.

3. **Continuous Monitoring**: Implement robust monitoring and alerting solutions to keep track of system performance and resource utilization. DevOps teams should receive real-time alerts when scaling actions are triggered.

4. **Test Scalability**: Perform load testing and stress testing to ensure that applications can handle expected traffic levels. Identify potential bottlenecks and address them in advance.

5. **Cost Analysis**: Continuously analyze cloud costs and resource utilization to identify opportunities for cost optimization. Make use of cloud provider tools and third-party cost management solutions.

Scaling and elasticity are integral components of DevOps practices in cloud environments, enabling organizations to meet user demands efficiently, maintain high availability, and optimize costs. By embracing these concepts, DevOps teams can ensure that applications perform reliably and adapt to changing workloads, ultimately delivering a better user experience.

9.4 Cloud Security Considerations for DevOps

Security is a paramount concern in DevOps, especially when operating in cloud environments. DevOps teams need to adopt a proactive approach to address security challenges effectively. In this section, we will explore the key considerations and best practices for ensuring cloud security within the DevOps lifecycle.

Shared Responsibility Model

Cloud providers typically follow a shared responsibility model, which outlines the division of security responsibilities between the cloud provider and the customer (DevOps team). While cloud providers are responsible for the security of the cloud infrastructure, customers are responsible for securing their applications and data.

Understanding this model is crucial for DevOps teams to delineate their responsibilities accurately and implement appropriate security measures.

Key Cloud Security Considerations

1. **Identity and Access Management (IAM)**: Implement strong IAM policies to control access to cloud resources. Ensure that only authorized personnel have access to critical assets. Use multi-factor authentication (MFA) to enhance security.
2. **Data Encryption**: Encrypt sensitive data at rest and in transit. Cloud providers offer encryption services and tools to protect data. DevOps teams should leverage these features to safeguard data.
3. **Compliance and Governance**: Ensure compliance with industry standards and regulations relevant to your

organization. Implement governance policies and regularly audit cloud resources to identify non-compliance.

4. **Security Patching**: Keep cloud resources up to date with security patches. DevOps teams should have automated processes in place to apply patches promptly.

5. **Network Security**: Implement network security best practices, including the use of firewalls, network segmentation, and intrusion detection systems (IDS). Limit exposure of resources to the public internet.

6. **Security Monitoring and Logging**: Set up continuous monitoring and logging for cloud resources. Use security information and event management (SIEM) solutions to detect and respond to security incidents in real time.

7. **Incident Response Plan**: Develop a robust incident response plan that outlines steps to take in case of a security breach or incident. Regularly test and update the plan to ensure its effectiveness.

8. **Backup and Disaster Recovery**: Implement backup and disaster recovery solutions to ensure data availability and business continuity. Regularly test data restoration processes.

Infrastructure as Code (IaC) Security

When using IaC to provision cloud resources, it's essential to consider security throughout the development and deployment stages. Some IaC-specific security considerations include:

1. **Secure Code Practices**: Follow secure coding practices when writing IaC templates to avoid vulnerabilities in infrastructure configurations.

2. **Template Validation**: Implement template validation processes to identify security issues and misconfigurations

before deploying resources.

3. **Secrets Management**: Safely manage and store secrets, such as API keys and passwords, using secure vaults or key management services provided by cloud providers.

4. **Code Repository Security**: Ensure that the repositories containing IaC code are secure. Implement access controls and monitor for code changes.

DevSecOps Integration

DevOps and security, often referred to as DevSecOps, should be tightly integrated throughout the software development lifecycle. Security checks and testing should be automated and performed continuously. This includes static application security testing (SAST), dynamic application security testing (DAST), and vulnerability scanning.

Continuous Security Improvement

Security in the cloud is an ongoing process. DevOps teams should embrace a culture of continuous security improvement. Regularly assess and update security measures, monitor for emerging threats, and stay informed about the latest security best practices and tools.

In conclusion, cloud security is a critical aspect of DevOps in cloud environments. DevOps teams must understand the shared responsibility model, implement security measures, and integrate security practices throughout the development and deployment processes. By following best practices and staying vigilant, DevOps teams can build and maintain secure and resilient cloud-based applications.

9.5 Case Studies: DevOps in Cloud

Environments

In this section, we will explore real-world case studies of organizations that have successfully adopted DevOps practices in cloud environments. These examples showcase how DevOps principles, combined with cloud computing, have led to improved agility, scalability, and efficiency.

Case Study 1: Netflix

Background: Netflix, the world's leading streaming entertainment service, has been a pioneer in adopting DevOps and cloud technologies to deliver content to millions of viewers globally.

DevOps and Cloud Integration: Netflix relies on Amazon Web Services (AWS) for its cloud infrastructure. The company uses a microservices architecture that enables continuous delivery and frequent updates. DevOps practices, such as automated testing and deployment, allow Netflix to release new features and content rapidly.

Benefits:

- **Scalability**: Netflix can scale its infrastructure up or down based on demand, ensuring a seamless streaming experience.

- **Resilience**: By using cloud-based redundancy and automated failover mechanisms, Netflix maintains high availability.

- **Personalization**: DevOps practices enable Netflix to personalize content recommendations for users, improving user satisfaction.

Case Study 2: Airbnb

Background: Airbnb, a global online marketplace for lodging and travel experiences, has embraced DevOps and cloud technology to manage its platform's growth.

DevOps and Cloud Integration: Airbnb utilizes Amazon Web Services (AWS) and Google Cloud Platform (GCP) for its cloud infrastructure. The company employs continuous integration and deployment to improve code quality and accelerate feature delivery. Automated testing and monitoring are crucial components of their DevOps strategy.

Benefits:

- **Rapid Innovation**: Airbnb can quickly develop and deploy new features, improving the user experience and staying ahead of competitors.

- **Cost Efficiency**: Cloud resources are optimized, allowing Airbnb to scale efficiently while controlling costs.

- **Global Reach**: DevOps practices enable Airbnb to serve users worldwide, with localized experiences and support.

Case Study 3: Adobe

Background: Adobe, a multinational software company known for its creative software products, has undergone a significant transformation by adopting DevOps and cloud technologies.

DevOps and Cloud Integration: Adobe utilizes Microsoft Azure for its cloud infrastructure. DevOps practices, including continuous integration, continuous delivery, and automated testing, have streamlined their software development processes. Adobe also embraces a culture of collaboration and feedback within cross-functional teams.

Benefits:

• **Faster Time to Market**: Adobe can release updates and new features more frequently, meeting customer demands faster.

• **Enhanced Collaboration**: DevOps fosters collaboration between development, operations, and quality assurance teams.

• **Improved Quality**: Automated testing and continuous feedback loops result in higher software quality.

Case Study 4: Capital One

Background: Capital One, a leading financial services company, has adopted DevOps practices and cloud technologies to drive digital transformation and deliver innovative financial solutions.

DevOps and Cloud Integration: Capital One leverages AWS for its cloud infrastructure. The company has embraced automation, including infrastructure as code (IaC), to provision and manage resources. DevOps practices have accelerated the deployment of secure and compliant applications.

Benefits:

• **Security and Compliance**: Capital One can enforce security and compliance policies across its cloud infrastructure, enhancing data protection.

- **Agility**: DevOps practices enable Capital One to respond quickly to market changes and customer needs.

- **Cost Management**: Cloud resources are optimized to control costs while maintaining scalability.

These case studies demonstrate the transformative power of DevOps in conjunction with cloud computing. Organizations across various industries can achieve increased agility, scalability, and efficiency while delivering high-quality products and services to their customers. DevOps and the cloud have become integral components of modern software development and operations strategies.

Chapter 10: Containerization and Orchestration

10.1 Introduction to Containers and Docker

In this section, we'll delve into the world of containerization and Docker, one of the most popular containerization platforms. Containerization has revolutionized how applications are packaged and deployed, offering numerous benefits in terms of portability, scalability, and consistency.

What are Containers?

Containers are lightweight, standalone executable packages that contain everything needed to run a piece of software, including the code, runtime, libraries, and system tools. Unlike traditional virtual machines (VMs), containers share the host operating system's kernel, making them highly efficient and resource-friendly.

Docker: A Leading Container Platform

Docker is a leading containerization platform that has played a pivotal role in popularizing container technology. It provides tools and a platform for building, shipping, and running containers. Here are some key aspects of Docker:

1. Images and Containers:

- **Images**: An image is a read-only template that contains the application's code, libraries, and dependencies. Images are used to create containers.

- **Containers**: A container is a runnable instance of an image. It encapsulates the application and its environment, ensuring consistency across different environments.

2. Docker Hub:

- **Docker Hub**: Docker Hub is a cloud-based repository where users can find and share Docker images. It offers a vast library of pre-built images for various software stacks.

3. Docker Compose:

- **Docker Compose**: Docker Compose is a tool for defining and running multi-container applications. It uses a YAML file to define the services, networks, and volumes required for a complete application stack.

Benefits of Containerization with Docker

Containerization, especially with Docker, offers several advantages:

1. Portability:

Containers are highly portable and can run consistently across different environments, from development to production. This eliminates the "it works on my machine" problem.

2. Scalability:

Containers can be easily scaled up or down to meet varying workloads. Container orchestration tools like Kubernetes facilitate automatic scaling based on demand.

3. Resource Efficiency:

Containers share the host's kernel and require less overhead compared to VMs, making them more resource-efficient.

4. Isolation:

Containers provide a level of process and filesystem isolation, ensuring that applications do not interfere with each other.

5. Rapid Deployment:

Containers can be spun up or torn down quickly, enabling rapid deployment and updates.

6. DevOps Integration:

Containers align well with DevOps practices, allowing for continuous integration, continuous deployment (CI/CD), and infrastructure as code (IaC).

Use Cases for Containers

Containers are versatile and find applications in various scenarios, including:

- **Microservices**: Containers are ideal for building and deploying microservices, where each service runs in its container.

- **Development and Testing**: Developers can use containers to create consistent development and testing environments.

- **CI/CD Pipelines**: Containers simplify the packaging and deployment of applications in CI/CD pipelines.

- **Legacy Application Modernization**: Containers can encapsulate and modernize legacy applications, making them more manageable.

Getting Started with Docker

To begin with Docker, you'll need to install it on your local machine or set up Docker on a server. Docker provides detailed installation guides for various platforms on its website.

Once Docker is installed, you can start creating Docker images, running containers, and exploring the vast Docker Hub repository for pre-built images.

In the following sections of this chapter, we'll explore more advanced topics related to containerization, including container orchestration with Kubernetes, best practices for container management, and the challenges of managing stateful applications in containers. Containerization has become a fundamental technology in the world of DevOps and modern software development, and understanding its principles is crucial for anyone involved in these fields.

10.2 Orchestration with Kubernetes

In this section, we'll explore Kubernetes, one of the most widely used container orchestration platforms. Kubernetes, often abbreviated as K8s, is an open-source container orchestration tool that automates the deployment, scaling, and management of containerized applications. It was originally developed by Google and is now maintained by the Cloud Native Computing Foundation (CNCF).

Key Concepts in Kubernetes

1. Nodes:

- In a Kubernetes cluster, a node is a physical or virtual machine that runs containerized applications. Each node is responsible for running containers and hosting services.

2. Pods:

- The smallest deployable unit in Kubernetes is called a pod. A pod can contain one or more containers that share the same network and storage namespace. Pods are co-located on the same node.

3. ReplicaSets:

- ReplicaSets are used to ensure that a specified number of pod replicas are running at all times. If a pod fails or is terminated, the ReplicaSet automatically replaces it.

4. Services:

- Kubernetes Services provide network connectivity and load balancing to pods. They abstract the network layer, making it easy to connect to pods without knowing their IP addresses.

5. Ingress:

- Ingress controllers and resources allow you to manage external access to services within a cluster. They are often used for routing external HTTP and HTTPS traffic to services.

6. ConfigMaps and Secrets:

- ConfigMaps and Secrets are used to manage configuration data and sensitive information separately from application code. They can be injected into pods as environment variables or mounted as files.

7. Volumes:

- Volumes are used for persistent storage in Kubernetes. They can be associated with pods to store data that persists even if the pod is terminated.

Why Use Kubernetes?

Kubernetes offers several advantages for container orchestration:

1. Scaling and Load Balancing:

- Kubernetes can automatically scale applications based on resource utilization, ensuring high availability and efficient resource utilization. It also provides built-in load balancing.

2. Self-Healing:

- Kubernetes monitors the health of pods and can automatically restart or replace failed instances, ensuring that applications are highly available.

3. Declarative Configuration:

- Configuration in Kubernetes is defined declaratively, which means you specify the desired state of your applications, and Kubernetes handles the details of achieving that state.

4. Rolling Updates and Rollbacks:

- Kubernetes supports rolling updates, allowing you to update application versions without downtime. If issues arise, you can easily roll back to a previous version.

5. Ecosystem and Community:

- Kubernetes has a vibrant ecosystem of tools and a large community, making it easy to find solutions to common challenges and leverage extensions.

Setting Up a Kubernetes Cluster

To get started with Kubernetes, you need to set up a Kubernetes cluster. You can do this on your local machine using tools like Minikube or on cloud providers like Google Kubernetes Engine (GKE), Amazon Elastic Kubernetes Service (EKS), or Microsoft Azure Kubernetes Service (AKS).

Here is a simplified example of deploying a simple Nginx web server using Kubernetes manifests:

apiVersion: v1

kind: Pod

metadata:

name: nginx-pod

spec:

containers:

- name: nginx-container

image: nginx:latest

You can create this YAML manifest using kubectl apply -f nginx-pod.yaml, and Kubernetes will create a pod running an Nginx container.

In upcoming chapters, we'll explore more advanced topics such as managing containerized applications in Kubernetes, deploying microservices, and using Helm for package management. Kubernetes has become a cornerstone of modern DevOps practices, enabling the efficient management of containerized applications at scale. Understanding its concepts and capabilities is essential for any DevOps engineer or software developer working with containers.

10.3 Containerization Best Practices

Containerization has become a fundamental technology in modern DevOps practices, and its adoption has skyrocketed with the rise of Kubernetes and Docker. While containers offer numerous benefits, it's crucial to follow best practices to ensure they are used effectively and securely.

1. Single Responsibility Principle:

- Each container should have a single responsibility. Avoid bundling multiple services or applications within a single container. This makes containers more maintainable and easier to scale.

2. Immutable Containers:

- Containers should be treated as immutable artifacts. Avoid making changes to a running container; instead, create a new version with the necessary updates. This promotes consistency and reproducibility.

3. Version Tagging:

- Always use version tags for container images (:latest should be avoided). Versioned images ensure that you can reproduce specific builds and deployments.

4. Minimal Base Images:

- Use minimal base images like Alpine Linux to reduce the attack surface and keep container sizes small. Avoid using bloated images with unnecessary packages.

5. Environment Configuration:

- Externalize configuration using environment variables or configuration files. Avoid hardcoding configuration inside container images.

6. Secrets Management:

- Use secrets management tools like Kubernetes Secrets or Docker Secrets for sensitive data like passwords and API keys. Never store secrets in container images.

7. Health Checks:

- Implement health checks in your containers to let orchestration platforms (e.g., Kubernetes) know when a container is ready to accept traffic.

8. Container Scanning:

- Regularly scan container images for vulnerabilities using tools like Clair, Trivy, or Anchore. This helps you identify and remediate security issues.

9. Resource Limits:

- Define resource limits (CPU and memory) for your containers to prevent resource contention and ensure predictable performance.

10. Logging and Monitoring:

- Implement logging and monitoring inside containers to capture application and system-level metrics. This helps in debugging and troubleshooting.

11. Container Orchestration:

- Use container orchestration platforms like Kubernetes to automate container deployment, scaling, and management. Orchestration tools simplify complex tasks.

12. Distributed Tracing:

- Consider implementing distributed tracing mechanisms (e.g., Jaeger, Zipkin) to trace requests across microservices, even in a containerized environment.

13. Caching and State Management:

- Understand the limitations of stateless containers and use appropriate caching mechanisms or databases for stateful applications.

14. Testing:

- Develop and maintain tests specifically for containerized applications to ensure they function correctly in the container environment.

15. Documentation:

- Create clear and up-to-date documentation for your containerized applications, including how to build, deploy, and configure them.

16. Backup and Disaster Recovery:

- Implement backup and disaster recovery strategies for your containerized data and configurations.

17. Container Registry Security:

- Secure your container registry to prevent unauthorized access and image tampering. Implement access controls and image signing.

18. Continuous Integration/Continuous Deployment (CI/CD):

- Integrate container builds into your CI/CD pipeline to automate image creation and deployment.

19. Networking:

- Understand the networking model of containers and ensure proper network segmentation and security policies.

20. Education and Training:

- Invest in training and educating your team on containerization best practices and security guidelines.

Following these containerization best practices helps ensure that your containerized applications are reliable, secure, and easy to manage. Containerization is a powerful technology when used correctly, and these practices are essential for a successful DevOps implementation.

10.4 Microservices and Containers

Microservices architecture and containerization are a match made in heaven. They complement each other's strengths and have become a popular choice for modern application development. In this section, we'll explore how microservices and containers work together and the benefits they bring to the world of DevOps.

Microservices Architecture:

Microservices is an architectural style that structures an application as a collection of small, independent services that can be developed, deployed, and scaled independently. Each service is responsible for a specific function, and they communicate through APIs or lightweight protocols.

Advantages of Microservices:

1. **Scalability**: Microservices can be scaled individually, allowing you to allocate resources efficiently based on demand.
2. **Flexibility**: Developers have the freedom to choose the right technology stack for each microservice, enabling innovation and faster development.
3. **Fault Isolation**: If one microservice fails, it doesn't necessarily affect the entire application. Faults are isolated, leading to better system resilience.
4. **Continuous Deployment**: Smaller codebases and independent services make it easier to implement continuous deployment pipelines.
5. **Team Autonomy**: Development teams can work independently on microservices, promoting agility and reducing dependencies.

Containerization and Microservices:

Containers provide a lightweight and consistent runtime environment for microservices. Here's how they complement each other:

1. **Isolation**: Containers isolate each microservice, ensuring that dependencies and libraries do not interfere with one another.
2. **Portability**: Microservices packaged as containers can run on any platform that supports containerization, making them highly portable.

3. **Resource Efficiency**: Containers are resource-efficient, allowing you to run multiple microservices on a single host without resource contention.
4. **Scaling**: Containers make it easy to scale individual microservices horizontally, responding to changing loads.
5. **Consistency**: Containers ensure that each microservice runs consistently across different environments, from development to production.

Challenges:

While microservices and containers offer significant benefits, they also introduce challenges:

1. **Complexity**: Managing a large number of microservices and containers can become complex, requiring robust orchestration and monitoring.
2. **Networking**: Ensuring secure and efficient communication between microservices can be challenging in a containerized environment.
3. **Data Management**: Handling databases and data storage in a microservices architecture can be complex and requires careful planning.
4. **Service Discovery**: Microservices need a way to discover and communicate with each other dynamically.

Best Practices:

To successfully implement microservices with containers, consider these best practices:

1. **Orchestration**: Use container orchestration platforms like Kubernetes to manage the deployment, scaling, and monitoring of microservices.

2. **API Gateways**: Implement an API gateway to manage external access to your microservices and to handle routing and authentication.

3. **Service Mesh**: Consider using a service mesh like Istio or Linkerd to address networking challenges, including load balancing, security, and observability.

4. **Observability**: Implement robust logging, monitoring, and tracing to gain insights into the behavior of microservices.

5. **Versioning**: Implement versioning for your APIs to ensure backward compatibility and facilitate gradual rollouts.

6. **Testing**: Develop comprehensive testing strategies, including unit, integration, and end-to-end testing, to validate the behavior of microservices.

Microservices and containers have reshaped how modern applications are developed and deployed. When implemented thoughtfully and with the right tools, they offer flexibility, scalability, and resilience, allowing organizations to deliver software faster and with greater reliability. However, they also come with their set of challenges that must be addressed effectively to reap the benefits fully.

10.5 Managing Stateful and Stateless Applications

In the world of microservices and containerization, applications can be broadly categorized into two types: stateful and stateless. Each type has its own characteristics, requirements, and challenges. In this section, we'll delve into the concepts of stateful and stateless applications and explore how to manage them effectively in a DevOps environment.

Stateful Applications:

Stateful applications, as the name suggests, maintain state information between interactions with clients or users. They store data that is specific to a particular user or session. Examples of stateful applications include traditional relational databases, in-memory caching systems, and some legacy monolithic applications.

Characteristics of Stateful Applications:

1. **Data Persistence**: Stateful applications rely on persistent data storage to maintain state information.
2. **Session Affinity**: They often require session affinity or sticky sessions to ensure that client requests are routed to the same instance that contains the user's data.
3. **Complex Scaling**: Scaling stateful applications can be complex due to the need to replicate or shard data across multiple instances.
4. **Recovery Challenges**: In case of failures, recovering stateful applications while preserving data consistency can be challenging.
5. **Resource Intensive**: Stateful applications tend to be more resource-intensive compared to their stateless counterparts.

Stateless Applications:

Stateless applications, on the other hand, do not maintain any session or user-specific data between requests. They treat each request independently and do not rely on local data storage. Stateless applications are designed for horizontal scalability and can be easily deployed and managed in containerized environments.

Characteristics of Stateless Applications:

1. **No Session State**: Stateless applications do not store session state on the server side, making them highly scalable and fault-tolerant.
2. **Stateless API**: RESTful APIs are often implemented in a stateless manner, allowing each request to contain all the necessary information.
3. **Elastic Scaling**: Stateless applications can be easily scaled horizontally by adding more instances as needed.
4. **Fault Tolerance**: Stateless services can recover from failures quickly, as they do not rely on preserving session state.

Managing Stateful Applications in Containers:

Containerizing stateful applications presents unique challenges:

1. **Data Persistence**: You must ensure that data is persistently stored and can be accessed by containerized instances. Solutions like container-attached storage (CAS) or network-attached storage (NAS) are commonly used.
2. **Data Backups**: Regular data backups and snapshotting mechanisms are crucial for safeguarding critical data.
3. **Stateful Sets**: Kubernetes provides StatefulSets to manage stateful applications. It ensures that each instance maintains a stable network identity and persistent storage.
4. **Scaling**: Scaling stateful applications can be complex, and care must be taken to maintain data consistency.

Managing Stateless Applications in Containers:

Stateless applications are inherently well-suited for containerization:

1. **Scalability**: Stateless applications can be easily scaled horizontally by deploying more container instances.

2. **Load Balancing**: Use load balancers or ingress controllers to distribute incoming traffic across container instances.

3. **Health Checks**: Implement health checks and automated recovery mechanisms to ensure high availability.

4. **Immutable Infrastructure**: Embrace the concept of immutable infrastructure, where container images are rebuilt for every change, ensuring consistency.

5. **Logs and Monitoring**: Implement robust logging and monitoring to gain insights into the behavior and performance of stateless applications.

In conclusion, managing stateful and stateless applications in containerized environments is a critical aspect of DevOps. It requires careful planning, the use of appropriate tools and technologies, and a deep understanding of the specific requirements of each application type. While stateful applications introduce complexities related to data persistence and recovery, stateless applications offer scalability and fault tolerance advantages. By addressing the unique challenges of each type effectively, DevOps teams can ensure the successful deployment and operation of both stateful and stateless applications in containerized environments.

Chapter 11: Microservices and DevOps

Microservices architecture has gained significant popularity in recent years due to its ability to break down large, monolithic applications into smaller, independently deployable services. This chapter explores the intersection of microservices and DevOps, focusing on how these two concepts complement each other and the challenges associated with deploying and managing microservices.

Section 11.1: Understanding Microservices Architecture

Microservices architecture represents a shift in software development towards building applications as a collection of loosely coupled services. This section provides an in-depth understanding of the key concepts and principles of microservices architecture.

Section 11.2: Aligning Microservices with DevOps Principles

DevOps practices can be seamlessly integrated into microservices development to enable faster delivery, better collaboration, and improved reliability. This section discusses how to align microservices projects with DevOps principles and practices.

Section 11.3: Challenges in Microservices Deployment

While microservices offer numerous advantages, they also come with their unique set of challenges, including service discovery, data consistency, and deployment complexities. This section explores these challenges and offers strategies for overcoming them.

Section 11.4: Monitoring and Managing Microservices

Effective monitoring and management of microservices are critical for ensuring their reliability and performance. This section covers the tools and techniques for monitoring and managing microservices in a DevOps environment.

Section 11.5: Case Studies: Transitioning to Microservices

Real-world case studies provide valuable insights into how organizations have successfully transitioned from monolithic architectures to microservices while implementing DevOps practices. This section presents these case studies to illustrate best practices and lessons learned.

Microservices and DevOps are at the forefront of modern software development, enabling organizations to deliver software faster and more reliably. Understanding the intricacies of microservices architecture and how to apply DevOps principles to microservices projects is crucial for staying competitive in today's software landscape. This chapter equips readers with the knowledge and tools necessary to navigate the world of microservices and DevOps effectively.

Chapter 11: Microservices and DevOps

Section 11.1: Understanding Microservices Architecture

Microservices architecture has emerged as a popular approach to designing and building software systems. It represents a departure from the traditional monolithic architecture and offers several advantages, including increased flexibility, scalability, and the ability to align more closely with DevOps principles. In this section, we will explore the core concepts of microservices architecture and how it differs from monolithic design.

What Are Microservices?

At its core, microservices architecture is an architectural style where an application is composed of loosely coupled, independently deployable services. These services are designed to be small, focused on specific business capabilities, and communicate with each other via well-defined APIs. Unlike monolithic applications, where all functionality is tightly integrated, microservices break down an application into smaller, manageable parts.

Key Characteristics of Microservices

Several key characteristics define microservices architecture:

1. **Decomposition**: Applications are decomposed into individual services, each responsible for a specific function or feature. This decomposition allows for easier management and scalability.
2. **Independence**: Microservices operate independently of each other. Each service can have its own technology stack, database, and development team, providing autonomy and flexibility.
3. **APIs**: Services communicate through APIs or network protocols. This standardized communication enables services to work together seamlessly while being developed and deployed independently.
4. **Scalability**: Microservices can be scaled independently based on demand. This fine-grained scalability is particularly useful for applications with varying workloads.
5. **Resilience**: Failure in one microservice does not necessarily impact the entire application. Redundancy and fault tolerance can be built into individual services.

Advantages of Microservices

Microservices architecture offers several advantages, making it an attractive choice for many organizations:

- **Flexibility**: Teams can choose the best technology stack for each service, allowing for innovation and optimization.

- **Scalability**: Services can be scaled individually, reducing the need for over-provisioning.

- **Faster Development**: Smaller, focused teams can develop and deploy services independently, accelerating the development process.

- **Easier Maintenance**: Isolating services simplifies maintenance, updates, and debugging.

- **Fault Isolation**: Failures in one service don't necessarily affect the entire application, enhancing overall reliability.

Microservices vs. Monolithic Architecture

To better understand microservices, it's essential to compare them with monolithic architecture:

- **Monolithic**: In a monolithic architecture, the entire application is a single, tightly integrated unit. Scaling and maintenance can be challenging, and changes to one part of the application may impact others.

- **Microservices**: Microservices break the application into smaller, manageable services that can be developed, deployed, and scaled independently. This modularity increases agility.

In summary, microservices architecture offers a more flexible and scalable approach to software development compared to traditional monolithic architecture. By understanding the fundamentals of microservices, organizations can harness their potential and leverage DevOps practices for faster and more reliable software delivery.

Section 11.2: Aligning Microservices with DevOps Principles

Microservices architecture and DevOps principles are highly complementary, and their alignment can lead to more efficient and effective software development and delivery. In this section, we will explore how microservices and DevOps work together, emphasizing their shared values and benefits.

Shared Values

Microservices and DevOps share several fundamental values that contribute to their synergy:

1. **Modularity**: Both microservices and DevOps promote modularity. Microservices are inherently modular by design, breaking down an application into smaller, independent components. DevOps focuses on modularizing the development and deployment pipeline, allowing for the independent integration of changes and features.

2. **Automation**: Automation is a core principle in DevOps. It streamlines repetitive tasks, reduces human error, and accelerates the delivery process. Microservices architecture

benefits from automation by allowing the independent deployment of services through automated pipelines.

3. **Continuous Integration and Continuous Deployment (CI/CD)**: CI/CD is a key DevOps practice that involves continuously integrating code changes, testing them, and deploying to production. Microservices, with their small and independent nature, are well-suited for CI/CD pipelines, enabling rapid and frequent releases.

4. **Scalability**: Both microservices and DevOps emphasize scalability. Microservices can be independently scaled to handle varying workloads, while DevOps practices enable the automation of scaling processes in response to changes in demand.

Benefits of Aligning Microservices and DevOps

When microservices architecture and DevOps principles are aligned, organizations can realize a range of benefits:

- **Faster Time to Market**: The combination of microservices' modularity and DevOps' automation results in quicker development cycles and faster delivery of features to end-users.

- **Improved Reliability**: Microservices' fault isolation and DevOps' automated testing and monitoring lead to improved system reliability. Failures in one service are less likely to impact the entire application.

- **Scalability**: DevOps practices enable the automated scaling of microservices based on real-time demand, ensuring optimal resource utilization.

- **Enhanced Collaboration**: Both microservices and DevOps encourage cross-functional collaboration. Development, operations, and quality assurance teams work closely together to deliver and maintain microservices.

- **Simplified Maintenance**: Independent microservices are easier to maintain and update. DevOps automation further simplifies the process of deploying updates without disrupting the entire application.

Challenges to Address

While aligning microservices with DevOps principles offers numerous advantages, there are also challenges to overcome:

- **Complexity**: Managing a microservices-based system can be more complex than a monolithic application, requiring careful coordination and monitoring.

- **Testing**: Testing in a microservices environment can be challenging due to the need for comprehensive integration testing and ensuring that all services work seamlessly together.

- **Monitoring**: Monitoring a distributed system of microservices requires robust tools and practices to gain visibility into each service's performance and troubleshoot issues effectively.

- **Security**: DevOps practices need to include security at every stage, and microservices introduce additional security considerations, such as securing communication between services.

- **Culture**: Transforming an organization to embrace both microservices and DevOps requires a cultural shift towards collaboration, automation, and shared responsibility.

In conclusion, aligning microservices architecture with DevOps principles can significantly benefit organizations seeking to improve their software development and delivery processes. While challenges exist, addressing them with the right tools, practices, and a culture of collaboration can lead to more agile, reliable, and scalable systems.

Section 11.3: Challenges in Microservices Deployment

While microservices offer many advantages, they also come with unique challenges, especially in the context of deployment. In this section, we'll explore some of the common challenges organizations face when deploying microservices-based applications.

1. Service Discovery and Communication

One of the fundamental challenges in a microservices architecture is enabling services to discover and communicate with each other. Unlike monolithic applications, where components can call each other directly, microservices may be distributed across various servers or containers. Implementing service discovery mechanisms, such as service registries and load balancers, is crucial to ensure seamless communication.

2. Data Management

Microservices often have their own data stores, which can lead to data management challenges. Maintaining data consistency, handling transactions across multiple services, and ensuring data availability are complex tasks. Organizations need to choose appropriate data storage solutions and implement strategies for data synchronization and sharing.

3. Deployment Automation

Microservices-based applications typically consist of many services that need to be independently deployed. Managing deployments manually is impractical, and organizations need robust automation tools and practices for continuous integration and continuous deployment (CI/CD). Container orchestration platforms like Kubernetes have become essential for automating microservices deployment and scaling.

4. Service Dependencies

Microservices often have interdependencies, where one service relies on another to fulfill its functionality. Managing these dependencies and ensuring that services are available when needed can be challenging. Circuit breakers, timeouts, and retries are common strategies to handle service failures gracefully.

5. Monitoring and Debugging

Monitoring a microservices-based application is complex due to the distributed nature of services. Organizations need effective monitoring solutions that provide visibility into the performance and health of each service. Additionally, debugging issues across services can be challenging, and distributed tracing tools are essential for diagnosing problems.

6. Security

Securing microservices is a multifaceted challenge. Organizations must secure communication between services, implement proper authentication and authorization mechanisms, and protect sensitive data. DevSecOps practices play a crucial role in integrating security into the development and deployment pipeline.

7. Versioning and Compatibility

As microservices evolve independently, managing versioning and ensuring backward compatibility becomes crucial. Organizations need to implement versioning strategies for APIs and services and have mechanisms in place to handle different versions in production.

8. Scalability

While microservices offer scalability benefits, effectively scaling services based on varying workloads can be challenging. Organizations need to implement auto-scaling strategies and monitor resource usage to ensure optimal performance.

9. Organizational Culture

Transitioning to a microservices architecture requires a cultural shift within an organization. Teams must adopt a DevOps mindset, embracing automation, collaboration, and shared responsibility. Cross-functional teams that include developers, operations, and quality assurance personnel are essential for successful microservices deployment.

10. Testing

Comprehensive testing in a microservices environment is critical. Teams must conduct extensive unit, integration, and end-to-end testing to ensure that all services work together seamlessly. Test automation is essential to maintain the rapid release cycles associated with microservices.

In conclusion, microservices offer flexibility and scalability but come with deployment challenges that organizations must address. Effective service discovery, data management, automation, and a strong focus on monitoring, security, and testing are essential for successful microservices deployment. Additionally, fostering a DevOps culture and embracing organizational changes are critical steps in overcoming these challenges and realizing the benefits of microservices architecture.

Section 11.4: Monitoring and Managing Microservices

Monitoring and managing microservices are essential aspects of ensuring the performance, reliability, and scalability of a microservices-based application. In this section, we'll delve into the strategies and tools organizations can use to effectively monitor and manage their microservices architecture.

1. Real-Time Monitoring

Real-time monitoring of microservices involves collecting and analyzing data about the health and performance of each service in real-time. Key metrics include response times, error rates, resource utilization, and service dependencies. Popular monitoring tools like Prometheus, Grafana, and Elasticsearch with Kibana provide dashboards and alerts to keep track of these metrics.

2. Distributed Tracing

Distributed tracing is crucial for understanding the flow of requests across microservices. It helps identify bottlenecks and performance issues by providing a detailed view of how requests traverse various services. Tools like Jaeger and Zipkin enable distributed tracing and can integrate with other monitoring solutions.

3. Centralized Logging

Centralized logging aggregates log data from all microservices into a central repository for analysis. Tools like the Elastic Stack (Elasticsearch, Logstash, and Kibana) and Splunk allow organizations to search, visualize, and analyze logs to troubleshoot issues and gain insights into application behavior.

4. Alerting and Notification

Setting up alerts and notifications is crucial to proactively identify and address issues. Monitoring tools often provide alerting capabilities based on predefined thresholds or anomaly detection algorithms. Alerts can be sent through various channels such as email, Slack, or SMS to notify the relevant teams.

5. Auto-Scaling

Auto-scaling ensures that microservices can handle varying workloads by automatically adjusting the number of instances based on predefined criteria. Container orchestration platforms like Kubernetes and cloud services like AWS Auto Scaling make it easier to implement auto-scaling strategies.

6. Load Balancing

Load balancing distributes incoming traffic evenly across multiple instances of a service to optimize performance and ensure high availability. Load balancers like NGINX and HAProxy can be deployed in front of microservices to manage traffic routing.

7. Service Mesh

Service mesh technologies like Istio and Linkerd provide features such as service discovery, load balancing, and security at the network level. They enable advanced traffic management and security policies, making it easier to manage microservices communication.

8. Performance Testing

Performance testing is essential to validate the scalability and responsiveness of microservices. Organizations should conduct load testing, stress testing, and capacity planning to ensure that services can handle expected loads and burst traffic.

9. Security Monitoring

Security should be an integral part of microservices monitoring. Detecting and responding to security threats, vulnerabilities, and anomalies is crucial. Tools like Falco and Sysdig provide runtime security monitoring and auditing capabilities for containers and microservices.

10. Capacity Planning

Capacity planning involves estimating future resource requirements based on historical data and expected growth. It helps ensure that there are sufficient resources available to support the application's needs without overprovisioning, which can be costly.

11. Continuous Improvement

Microservices monitoring should not be a static process. Organizations should continuously analyze monitoring data, identify areas for improvement, and optimize the architecture, performance, and resource allocation of microservices.

12. Chaos Engineering

Chaos engineering involves intentionally introducing failures and chaos into a microservices environment to test its resilience and identify weaknesses. Tools like Chaos Monkey and Gremlin help organizations conduct controlled experiments to improve system reliability.

In summary, effective monitoring and management of microservices require a combination of real-time monitoring, distributed tracing, centralized logging, alerting, auto-scaling, load balancing, and security practices. Continuous improvement through capacity planning and chaos engineering ensures that microservices-based applications remain robust and resilient in a dynamic and distributed environment.

Section 11.5: Case Studies: Transitioning to Microservices

In this section, we will explore real-world case studies of organizations that successfully transitioned to microservices architectures. These examples demonstrate the challenges they faced, the strategies they employed, and the benefits they achieved through microservices adoption.

1. Netflix

Challenge: Netflix faced scalability and deployment challenges with its monolithic application. The growth of its user base and content catalog necessitated a more flexible and efficient architecture.

Strategy: Netflix transitioned to a microservices-based architecture, known as the "Netflix OSS" stack. They decomposed their monolithic application into hundreds of microservices, each responsible for specific functions like recommendation, playback, and user management. They also embraced DevOps practices for faster development and deployment.

Benefits: Netflix achieved greater scalability, resilience, and the ability to roll out new features faster. Their microservices architecture enables personalized recommendations, fault tolerance, and smooth streaming experiences for millions of users worldwide.

2. Amazon

Challenge: Amazon faced challenges in managing its rapidly growing e-commerce platform. They needed to improve development speed, reduce downtime, and enhance the customer shopping experience.

Strategy: Amazon adopted a microservices architecture to break down their monolithic application into smaller, more manageable services. They also leveraged containerization and AWS services for scalability and resource optimization. Amazon heavily invested in automation and CI/CD pipelines to accelerate development and reduce manual interventions.

Benefits: Amazon's microservices approach enabled them to deploy new features and updates continuously. It also improved fault isolation, allowing failures in one service to have minimal impact on the overall system. This architecture has contributed to Amazon's position as a leader in e-commerce.

3. Uber

Challenge: Uber needed to expand rapidly to meet global demand. Their monolithic application struggled to scale efficiently and maintain a consistent user experience.

Strategy: Uber adopted microservices to decentralize their application, allowing individual teams to build and deploy their services independently. They also invested in tools like Apache Kafka for event-driven communication between services. Uber embraced a culture of experimentation, where developers were encouraged to innovate and own their services.

Benefits: Microservices allowed Uber to expand globally while maintaining a seamless user experience. It also enabled the development of new features and services at a faster pace. Uber's microservices architecture supports real-time tracking, pricing, and driver-partner experiences.

4. Airbnb

Challenge: Airbnb wanted to enhance the experience for hosts and guests on their platform. Their monolithic application made it challenging to iterate quickly and introduce new features.

Strategy: Airbnb shifted to a microservices architecture, focusing on domain-driven design principles. They broke down their monolithic application into services related to core business domains like booking, payment, and search. Airbnb also adopted GraphQL to enable efficient and flexible data retrieval.

Benefits: Airbnb's microservices approach allowed them to innovate rapidly, delivering features that improved user experiences for both hosts and guests. Their services are scalable, allowing them to handle a diverse range of property listings and booking requests.

5. Spotify

Challenge: Spotify aimed to provide a personalized music streaming experience to millions of users. They needed a scalable and flexible architecture to handle their massive catalog and user base.

Strategy: Spotify adopted a microservices-based architecture called the "Spotify Model." They organized teams into "Squads" that owned specific features or services. These squads had autonomy in their technology choices and development processes. Spotify also invested in cross-squad collaboration and alignment.

Benefits: The Spotify Model allowed Spotify to continuously innovate and personalize recommendations and playlists for users. The microservices architecture enables efficient content delivery and streaming, making it one of the world's leading music streaming platforms.

These case studies highlight the diverse ways organizations can successfully transition to microservices, leading to improved scalability, faster innovation, and enhanced user experiences. While the journey may involve challenges, the benefits of microservices adoption are evident in these industry leaders' success stories.

Chapter 12: Scaling DevOps Practices

Section 12.1: Strategies for Scaling DevOps in Large Organizations

Scaling DevOps practices in large organizations presents unique challenges and opportunities. While DevOps principles emphasize collaboration, automation, and cultural alignment, these principles must adapt to the scale and complexity of enterprise-level operations. In this section, we will explore strategies and best practices for effectively scaling DevOps in large organizations.

Challenges in Scaling DevOps

Large organizations face several challenges when scaling DevOps:

1. **Complexity:** Enterprise-scale operations involve numerous teams, applications, and technologies. Coordinating these elements can be complex, leading to bottlenecks and inefficiencies.
2. **Cultural Resistance:** Cultural transformation becomes more challenging as organizations grow. Teams and individuals may resist changes to established processes and hierarchies.
3. **Compliance and Security:** Meeting regulatory compliance and security standards becomes more critical and complex at scale. DevOps practices must ensure both speed and security.
4. **Communication:** Effective communication can become more difficult as teams and departments grow, leading to silos and information gaps.

Strategies for Scaling DevOps

To overcome these challenges and scale DevOps effectively, organizations can implement the following strategies:

1. **Executive Support:** Strong executive support is crucial for driving cultural change and resource allocation. Leaders should advocate for DevOps principles and invest in training and resources.
2. **Standardization:** Implement standardized DevOps practices and tools across the organization. This reduces complexity and ensures consistency.
3. **Collaboration:** Promote collaboration across teams and departments. Cross-functional teams can break down silos and improve communication.
4. **Automation:** Invest in automation for repetitive tasks, including deployment, testing, and monitoring. Automation enhances efficiency and reduces errors.
5. **DevOps as a Service:** Establish DevOps as a centralized service that provides tools, best practices, and support to internal teams. This approach centralizes expertise and promotes consistency.
6. **Scaling Agile:** If your organization uses Agile methodologies, align DevOps practices with Agile principles to foster collaboration and continuous improvement.
7. **Measurement and Metrics:** Implement metrics and key performance indicators (KPIs) to track progress and identify areas for improvement. Data-driven decision-making is essential at scale.
8. **Education and Training:** Offer DevOps training and resources to all teams, from development and testing to operations and security. Ensure that everyone understands

and embraces DevOps principles.

9. **Start Small:** Begin scaling efforts with a specific project or team to pilot new practices and tools. Once proven successful, expand to other areas of the organization.

10. **Feedback Loops:** Continuously collect feedback from teams and stakeholders to identify pain points and areas for improvement. Feedback loops are essential for adaptive scaling.

Case Studies

Several large organizations have successfully scaled DevOps practices. For example, Microsoft, a technology giant, adopted DevOps across its organization, leading to faster development cycles and improved product quality. Similarly, Capital One, a financial services company, scaled DevOps to deliver applications and services more rapidly while ensuring compliance with strict security and regulatory requirements.

In conclusion, scaling DevOps practices in large organizations requires a combination of cultural, technical, and organizational changes. By addressing challenges, fostering collaboration, and embracing automation, enterprises can successfully scale DevOps and reap the benefits of faster, more reliable software delivery.

Section 12.2: Handling Multi-Team Coordination and Collaboration

In large organizations, multi-team coordination and collaboration are pivotal for scaling DevOps effectively. When multiple teams are involved in software development and delivery, seamless collaboration becomes essential to maintain agility and ensure successful outcomes. This section explores strategies for handling multi-team coordination and fostering collaboration in a DevOps environment.

Challenges in Multi-Team Collaboration

Handling multi-team collaboration can be challenging due to various factors:

1. **Silos and Specialization:** Teams may operate in silos with specialized roles and responsibilities. This can hinder cross-functional collaboration.
2. **Communication Barriers:** Large organizations often have distributed teams and geographical barriers, leading to communication challenges.
3. **Conflicting Priorities:** Different teams may have conflicting priorities, making it difficult to align on common goals.
4. **Toolchain Complexity:** Each team may use its set of tools and technologies, leading to toolchain complexity and interoperability issues.

Strategies for Effective Multi-Team Collaboration

To overcome these challenges, organizations should implement strategies for effective multi-team collaboration in their DevOps initiatives:

1. **Cross-Functional Teams:** Form cross-functional teams that include members from development, testing, operations, and other relevant departments. These teams collaborate on end-to-end product delivery.
2. **Shared Goals:** Define and communicate shared goals and objectives across teams. Ensure that everyone understands how their work contributes to the overall success of the

project.

3. **Clear Communication:** Establish clear communication channels and practices. Regular meetings, video conferences, and collaboration tools can facilitate communication among distributed teams.

4. **DevOps Champions:** Appoint DevOps champions or advocates within each team who can promote DevOps principles, best practices, and collaboration within their respective groups.

5. **Common Tooling:** Standardize the toolset used across teams where possible. This reduces toolchain complexity and enhances interoperability.

6. **Automation and Integration:** Automate processes and integrate tools to streamline workflows. For example, automate the deployment pipeline to ensure consistent and repeatable deployments.

7. **Feedback Loops:** Implement feedback loops between teams to provide early visibility into issues and improvements. Encourage a culture of constructive feedback.

8. **Knowledge Sharing:** Facilitate knowledge sharing sessions and workshops among teams. Cross-training team members can promote a better understanding of each other's roles and responsibilities.

9. **Conflict Resolution:** Establish mechanisms for conflict resolution and decision-making. Clearly define how conflicts will be addressed to maintain collaboration.

10. **Metrics and Performance Monitoring:** Use metrics and performance monitoring to track the progress of multi-team collaboration efforts. Identify areas that need improvement and celebrate successes.

Case Studies

Several organizations have successfully tackled multi-team collaboration challenges in their DevOps journeys. Amazon Web Services (AWS) emphasizes the use of two-pizza teams, where a team should be small enough that it can be fed with two pizzas. This encourages small, cross-functional teams that can work efficiently and collaboratively. Similarly, Netflix, known for its DevOps practices, empowers its teams to operate independently while providing them with the necessary tools and resources for collaboration.

In summary, handling multi-team coordination and collaboration is vital for scaling DevOps in large organizations. By addressing communication barriers, aligning on shared goals, and fostering cross-functional teams, organizations can navigate the complexities of multi-team collaboration and achieve successful DevOps outcomes.

Section 12.3: Resource Management and Optimization

Efficient resource management and optimization are crucial aspects of scaling DevOps practices in large organizations. As teams collaborate on complex projects, they must ensure that resources such as hardware, cloud resources, and software licenses are used optimally to achieve cost-effectiveness and maintain agility.

Challenges in Resource Management

Large organizations often face several resource management challenges in their DevOps initiatives:

1. **Resource Sprawl:** With multiple teams and projects, there

is a risk of resource sprawl, where resources are underutilized, leading to increased costs.

2. **Budget Constraints:** Limited budgets require organizations to optimize resource allocation to achieve maximum value from their investments.

3. **Resource Conflicts:** Different teams may compete for the same resources, causing conflicts and inefficiencies.

4. **Capacity Planning:** Predicting resource needs and scaling infrastructure accordingly can be challenging, resulting in either under-provisioning or over-provisioning.

Strategies for Resource Management and Optimization

To address these challenges and ensure efficient resource management, organizations can implement the following strategies:

1. **Resource Visibility:** Gain visibility into all resources used across teams and projects. Utilize resource management tools and dashboards to track usage.

2. **Resource Tagging:** Implement a tagging system to categorize and label resources. This helps in identifying resource owners, project affiliations, and cost centers.

3. **Cost Allocation:** Allocate costs to specific teams or projects based on resource usage. This encourages accountability and transparency.

4. **Resource Right-Sizing:** Regularly review and right-size resources. Identify over-provisioned or underutilized resources and adjust configurations accordingly.

5. **Automation:** Automate resource provisioning and de-provisioning processes. Use infrastructure as code (IaC) and cloud automation tools to scale resources based on demand.

6. **Reserved Instances:** In cloud environments, leverage reserved instances to reduce costs for long-term resource commitments.

7. **Resource Governance:** Establish resource governance policies and guidelines. Ensure that teams adhere to resource allocation and optimization best practices.

8. **Capacity Planning:** Use historical data and predictive analytics to plan resource capacity. Anticipate future needs and scale resources proactively.

9. **Collaborative Resource Planning:** Encourage cross-team collaboration in resource planning. Centralize resource allocation decisions to prevent conflicts.

10. **Cost Monitoring:** Continuously monitor resource costs and analyze cost trends. Identify opportunities for cost reduction and optimization.

Case Studies

Companies like Netflix and Google have implemented resource management and optimization strategies effectively. Netflix's Simian Army, a suite of tools for testing and improving the resilience of its cloud infrastructure, includes tools for resource management and optimization. Google Cloud offers cost management tools and recommendations to help organizations optimize their cloud spending.

In conclusion, resource management and optimization are essential for achieving cost-effectiveness and agility in DevOps at scale. By implementing visibility, automation, cost allocation, and collaborative resource planning, organizations can successfully manage resources in large-scale DevOps initiatives.

Section 12.4: Overcoming Challenges in

Scaling

Scaling DevOps practices in large organizations comes with a unique set of challenges that need to be addressed to ensure successful implementation. These challenges are often complex and multifaceted, requiring careful planning and execution. In this section, we'll explore some common challenges and strategies for overcoming them.

Challenge 1: Coordination and Collaboration

In large organizations with multiple teams and departments, coordination and collaboration can become challenging. Teams may have different processes, tools, and priorities, making it difficult to align efforts.

Strategy: Implement cross-functional teams and establish clear communication channels. Use collaboration tools and platforms that facilitate real-time communication and document sharing. Regularly hold cross-team meetings and workshops to foster collaboration.

Challenge 2: Resource Constraints

Resource constraints, such as limited budgets and personnel, can hinder the scaling of DevOps practices. Large organizations often have to allocate resources carefully to meet project demands.

Strategy: Prioritize projects based on business impact and strategic goals. Advocate for increased budget allocation for critical DevOps initiatives. Consider outsourcing or partnering with third-party vendors when resources are limited.

Challenge 3: Legacy Systems

Legacy systems and applications can pose a significant challenge when scaling DevOps. These systems may have outdated technologies and dependencies that are difficult to integrate into modern DevOps pipelines.

Strategy: Invest in modernization efforts to update and refactor legacy systems gradually. Implement bridge solutions or wrappers to integrate legacy components with DevOps pipelines. Prioritize legacy system upgrades to align with DevOps practices.

Challenge 4: Compliance and Security

Maintaining compliance and security standards becomes more complex as DevOps scales in a large organization. Ensuring that all processes and practices adhere to regulatory requirements is critical.

Strategy: Establish a DevSecOps culture that integrates security into the DevOps lifecycle. Implement automated security testing and compliance checks. Collaborate with compliance and security teams to develop clear guidelines and standards.

Challenge 5: Resistance to Change

Resistance to change is a common challenge when scaling DevOps. Employees may be accustomed to traditional processes and may resist adopting new DevOps practices.

Strategy: Provide comprehensive training and education programs to help employees understand the benefits of DevOps. Involve teams in the decision-making process to address concerns and gather feedback. Showcase success stories and positive outcomes from DevOps initiatives.

Challenge 6: Maintaining Quality

Maintaining software quality while scaling DevOps practices is essential. Rapid development and deployment can sometimes lead to quality issues if not managed effectively.

Strategy: Implement automated testing and continuous integration practices to catch defects early in the development process. Establish strict quality gates and conduct thorough testing before production deployment. Use monitoring and feedback loops to identify and resolve quality issues in real-time.

Challenge 7: Scaling Culture

Maintaining a DevOps culture that values collaboration, transparency, and continuous improvement can be challenging as organizations grow larger.

Strategy: Continuously reinforce the DevOps culture through leadership support and role modeling. Celebrate successes and recognize individuals and teams for their contributions to the culture. Encourage a learning and feedback-oriented culture.

Challenge 8: Measurement and Metrics

Measuring the effectiveness and impact of DevOps practices at scale requires robust metrics and measurement systems. Inaccurate or incomplete metrics can lead to misinformed decisions.

Strategy: Define key performance indicators (KPIs) and metrics that align with organizational goals. Implement automated monitoring and measurement tools to gather data. Regularly review and analyze metrics to identify areas for improvement.

In conclusion, scaling DevOps practices in large organizations involves addressing a variety of challenges related to coordination, resources, legacy systems, compliance, culture, and more. By implementing the strategies outlined above, organizations can overcome these challenges and successfully scale DevOps to achieve agility, efficiency, and innovation at scale.

Section 12.5: Success Stories of DevOps at Scale

Scaling DevOps practices in large organizations has led to numerous success stories, demonstrating the transformative power of DevOps in delivering value, increasing efficiency, and achieving innovation at scale. In this section, we will explore some notable success stories from various industries and sectors.

1. Netflix

Netflix is a prime example of a company that has successfully embraced DevOps at scale. They have transitioned from a traditional monolithic architecture to a microservices-based approach, allowing them to release new features and updates rapidly. Netflix relies on a robust DevOps pipeline, automated testing, and continuous deployment to ensure a seamless streaming experience for millions of users worldwide.

2. Amazon Web Services (AWS)

Amazon Web Services, one of the world's leading cloud service providers, practices DevOps principles extensively. AWS enables organizations of all sizes to scale their infrastructure and applications effortlessly. They provide a wide range of DevOps tools and services, including AWS CodePipeline and AWS CodeDeploy, to help businesses achieve continuous integration and continuous delivery.

3. Target

Retail giant Target has embraced DevOps to enhance its e-commerce platform. By implementing DevOps practices, Target has improved its software delivery speed and quality. They have also automated infrastructure provisioning and use infrastructure as code (IaC) to manage their cloud resources efficiently.

4. Microsoft

Microsoft, a technology behemoth, has been on a journey to adopt DevOps across its vast product ecosystem. Azure DevOps, an integrated set of DevOps services offered by Microsoft, helps teams plan, develop, test, and deliver software efficiently. This has allowed Microsoft to accelerate its product development cycles and deliver updates and security patches more quickly.

5. Capital One

Capital One, a leading financial institution, has been a pioneer in adopting DevOps in the banking sector. They have embraced DevOps practices to accelerate application development and improve security. Capital One's journey involves automation, continuous integration, and a strong focus on security, allowing them to deliver features to customers faster while ensuring data protection.

6. Google

Google, known for its innovative approach to technology, has integrated DevOps practices into its software development and operations. Google Cloud offers a range of DevOps tools, such as Google Kubernetes Engine (GKE), which simplifies container orchestration and management. Google's experience with large-scale infrastructure has contributed to the development of many DevOps best practices.

7. Etsy

Etsy, an online marketplace for handmade and vintage goods, relies heavily on DevOps to manage its e-commerce platform. They have automated deployment pipelines, real-time monitoring, and proactive incident response strategies in place. Etsy's commitment to DevOps has resulted in improved site reliability and faster feature delivery.

8. Facebook

Facebook, one of the world's largest social media platforms, practices DevOps to manage its infrastructure and services at scale. They utilize technologies like Chef and Puppet for configuration management and automation. Continuous deployment and automated testing ensure that new features are rolled out seamlessly to billions of users.

These success stories highlight that DevOps is not limited to specific industries but can be applied across various sectors to achieve remarkable results. The key to DevOps success at scale lies in fostering a culture of collaboration, automation, and continuous improvement while leveraging the right tools and technologies. These organizations serve as inspiration for others looking to embark on their DevOps journeys and scale their operations effectively.

Section 13.1: Key Performance Indicators in

DevOps

Key Performance Indicators (KPIs) play a crucial role in measuring the success of DevOps practices and processes. They provide quantifiable data that helps organizations evaluate their performance, identify areas for improvement, and make informed decisions. In the context of DevOps, KPIs help teams assess their ability to deliver software efficiently and reliably. Let's explore some of the essential KPIs in DevOps:

1. Deployment Frequency

Deployment frequency measures how often code changes are deployed to production. It reflects an organization's agility and ability to respond quickly to user demands and market changes. High deployment frequency is often associated with successful DevOps practices, as it allows for faster feature delivery and bug fixes.

2. Lead Time for Changes

Lead time for changes represents the time it takes to implement and deliver a new feature, bug fix, or enhancement from the initial idea to production deployment. Short lead times indicate efficient development and delivery processes, enabling organizations to respond rapidly to customer needs.

3. Change Failure Rate

Change failure rate calculates the percentage of code changes that result in failures or issues after deployment. A low change failure rate indicates the stability and reliability of an organization's software delivery pipeline. It reflects the effectiveness of testing, quality control, and risk management practices.

4. Mean Time to Recovery (MTTR)

MTTR measures the average time it takes to restore a service or application to normal operation after a failure or incident. A lower MTTR indicates that teams can identify and resolve issues quickly, minimizing downtime and user impact. Efficient incident management and automated recovery processes contribute to a lower MTTR.

5. Availability and Reliability

Availability and reliability KPIs measure the percentage of time that a system or service is available and operational. High availability and reliability are essential for delivering a seamless user experience. These metrics help organizations assess the effectiveness of their infrastructure, monitoring, and fault tolerance strategies.

6. Customer Satisfaction

Customer satisfaction is a vital KPI that reflects how well an organization's software meets user expectations. Feedback from users, surveys, and Net Promoter Scores (NPS) can provide insights into user satisfaction. Improving customer satisfaction is a fundamental goal of DevOps, as it drives user loyalty and business success.

7. Code Quality Metrics

Code quality metrics, such as code coverage, code complexity, and static code analysis results, help teams assess the maintainability and reliability of their codebase. These metrics contribute to the overall health of the software and can guide efforts to refactor and improve code quality.

8. Infrastructure Utilization

Infrastructure utilization measures the efficiency of resource allocation in a cloud or data center environment. It includes metrics like CPU utilization, memory usage, and network bandwidth. Optimizing infrastructure utilization helps reduce costs and ensures efficient resource allocation.

9. Work in Progress (WIP)

WIP limits and metrics help teams manage their workloads and prevent overloading. Tracking the number of concurrent tasks or user stories in progress can improve workflow efficiency and reduce bottlenecks in the development process.

10. DevOps Culture Metrics

Cultural KPIs assess the adoption of DevOps principles and practices within an organization. They may include metrics related to collaboration, knowledge sharing, and cross-functional teamwork. Creating a DevOps culture is critical for success, and these metrics help gauge cultural transformation progress.

Selecting and tracking the right KPIs is essential for monitoring and improving DevOps initiatives. Organizations should align KPIs with their specific goals, regularly review performance data, and use insights to drive continuous improvement. Effective KPI monitoring ensures that DevOps practices remain focused on delivering value, improving quality, and accelerating software delivery.

Section 13.2: Measuring Deployment Frequency and Success Rates

Measuring deployment frequency and success rates is essential in DevOps to assess the efficiency and reliability of the software delivery pipeline. These key performance indicators (KPIs) provide insights into how frequently code changes are deployed and how often those deployments result in successful outcomes. Let's delve deeper into these two critical metrics:

Deployment Frequency

Deployment frequency, also known as release frequency, quantifies how often code changes are pushed into production. This KPI helps organizations understand their ability to deliver new features, enhancements, and bug fixes rapidly. A high deployment frequency is often indicative of efficient DevOps practices.

To measure deployment frequency, consider the following aspects:

1. **Frequency of Deployments**: Calculate how many deployments occur in a given timeframe, such as per day, week, or month. This gives you an idea of the release cadence.

2. **Time to Deploy**: Measure the time it takes from the completion of a code change to its deployment in a production environment. Shorter times indicate faster delivery.

3. **Release Triggers**: Identify the triggers that initiate deployments, such as code commits, pull requests, or automated pipelines. Understanding the release process is crucial for optimizing it.

4. **Deployment Automation**: Assess the extent to which deployments are automated. Automation reduces manual

intervention and accelerates deployment frequency.

Success Rate of Deployments

The success rate of deployments measures the percentage of deployments that result in successful outcomes. A successful deployment is one where the changes are implemented without causing critical issues, disruptions, or rollbacks. High success rates indicate a stable and reliable software delivery process.

To measure the success rate of deployments, consider the following factors:

1. **Deployment Failures**: Track the number of deployments that encounter issues or failures during or after deployment. Identify the root causes of failures.
2. **Rollback Frequency**: Monitor how often rollbacks are necessary due to deployment problems. Frequent rollbacks indicate challenges in maintaining system stability.
3. **Incident Response**: Assess how quickly incidents or issues resulting from deployments are detected, acknowledged, and resolved. A swift incident response minimizes downtime.
4. **User Feedback**: Gather user feedback to evaluate the impact of deployments on the end-user experience. Positive feedback suggests successful deployments, while negative feedback may indicate issues.
5. **Testing Practices**: Evaluate the effectiveness of testing practices, including automated testing, integration testing, and user acceptance testing, in ensuring successful deployments.

In addition to these metrics, organizations often use tools and dashboards to visualize deployment frequency and success rates. Continuous monitoring and analysis of these KPIs enable teams to identify areas for improvement, enhance automation, and optimize their DevOps processes.

Overall, deployment frequency and success rates are critical KPIs that reflect an organization's ability to deliver software quickly and reliably, meeting the demands of both customers and the market. Tracking these metrics is fundamental to the continuous improvement of DevOps practices and the achievement of business objectives.

Section 13.3: Tracking Lead Time and Change Failure Rate

Tracking lead time and change failure rate are essential aspects of measuring and optimizing the software delivery process in a DevOps environment. These key performance indicators (KPIs) provide valuable insights into the efficiency and reliability of the development and deployment pipeline.

Lead Time

Lead time, often referred to as cycle time, represents the duration it takes for a code change, from its inception (e.g., a new feature request or bug report) to its deployment into a production environment. It encompasses all the stages of development, including coding, testing, reviewing, and deploying.

Measuring lead time helps organizations:

1. **Identify Bottlenecks**: By breaking down the lead time into its constituent parts, teams can pinpoint bottlenecks or

delays in the development process, allowing for focused improvement efforts.

2. **Predict Delivery Dates**: Understanding the average lead time enables more accurate prediction of when a requested feature or bug fix will be delivered to end-users.

3. **Optimize Workflow**: Analyzing lead time data helps streamline workflows and improve process efficiency, ultimately reducing the time it takes to deliver value to customers.

4. **Improve Communication**: Teams can use lead time data to communicate expectations with stakeholders more effectively, enhancing transparency and trust.

Change Failure Rate

Change failure rate (CFR) represents the percentage of code changes or deployments that result in failure, causing disruptions, incidents, or rollbacks. A high CFR indicates instability in the software delivery process, which can lead to reduced customer satisfaction and operational challenges.

To calculate CFR, organizations can follow these steps:

1. **Count Failures**: Keep track of the number of deployments or code changes that encounter issues, whether technical or functional.

2. **Count Total Changes**: Determine the total number of deployments or code changes during the same timeframe.

3. **Calculate CFR**: Divide the number of failures by the total changes and multiply by 100 to get the CFR as a percentage.

A lower CFR is desirable, indicating a more stable and reliable software delivery process. DevOps teams should continuously work to reduce CFR through practices such as automated testing, thorough validation, and improved rollback strategies.

Using Lead Time and CFR Together

Lead time and CFR are often used in conjunction to assess the overall health of the software delivery pipeline. A shorter lead time and a lower CFR indicate that code changes are not only delivered faster but also with higher reliability.

It's important to note that lead time and CFR can vary based on the complexity of code changes, the quality of testing and validation processes, and the overall maturity of the DevOps practices within an organization. Regularly monitoring and analyzing these KPIs can help teams identify areas for improvement and refine their DevOps processes to deliver value more efficiently and reliably.

Section 13.4: Using Metrics for Continuous Improvement

In the world of DevOps, metrics play a pivotal role in driving continuous improvement. These metrics help organizations assess the effectiveness of their DevOps practices, identify areas that need enhancement, and make data-driven decisions to optimize their software delivery pipelines.

Key Metrics for Continuous Improvement

1. Lead Time and Cycle Time: As discussed in the previous section (13.3), lead time and cycle time are essential metrics that reveal how long it takes to deliver code changes from inception to production. *By tracking these metrics, teams can spot inefficiencies and streamline their development processes.*

2. *Deployment Frequency: Deployment frequency measures how often code changes are released into production. Increasing deployment frequency is a common DevOps goal, as it allows organizations to deliver new features and fixes more rapidly. However, it should be balanced with other metrics to ensure stability.*

3. *Change Failure Rate (CFR): CFR, also mentioned earlier, indicates the percentage of code changes that result in failures. Lowering CFR is crucial for improving software reliability and reducing disruptions.*

4. *Mean Time to Recovery (MTTR): MTTR quantifies the average time it takes to recover from an incident or failure in production. Reducing MTTR ensures that issues are resolved more swiftly, minimizing downtime and customer impact.*

5. *Availability and Uptime: Monitoring the availability and uptime of applications and services is essential for ensuring a positive user experience. Metrics related to availability help teams proactively address issues before they impact users.*

6. *Incident Response Time: This metric measures how quickly the team responds to incidents or alerts. A shorter incident response time is crucial for minimizing the impact of incidents on users.*

7. *Customer Satisfaction (CSAT) and Net Promoter Score (NPS): While not technical metrics, CSAT and NPS gauge customer satisfaction and loyalty. They provide valuable feedback on the*

quality of the product and user experience.

Continuous Improvement Process

Continuous improvement in DevOps is an iterative process that involves the following steps:

1. **Define Objectives**: Clearly define the goals and objectives you want to achieve, such as reducing lead time, increasing deployment frequency, or lowering CFR.
2. **Measure Baseline**: Establish a baseline by measuring the current state of relevant metrics. This provides a starting point for improvement efforts.
3. **Identify Areas for Improvement**: Analyze the baseline data to identify areas that require improvement. Look for bottlenecks, inefficiencies, or patterns of failure.
4. **Implement Changes**: Implement changes, whether they involve process optimizations, automation, or infrastructure enhancements. Changes should be aligned with the defined objectives.
5. **Monitor and Measure**: Continuously monitor and measure the impact of the implemented changes. Use the same metrics to assess whether improvements are being realized.
6. **Iterate**: Based on the data and feedback, iterate on your improvements. DevOps is a cyclical process, and continuous refinement is key to ongoing success.
7. **Share Insights**: Share insights and improvements with the broader team. Effective communication ensures that everyone is aligned and can contribute to the continuous improvement process.
8. **Celebrate Successes**: Recognize and celebrate successes, both small and large. Positive reinforcement motivates

teams to continue striving for improvement.

Tools and Automation

To facilitate the measurement and monitoring of these metrics, organizations often leverage various DevOps tools and automation solutions. These tools can collect, analyze, and visualize data, making it easier to track progress and identify trends over time.

In summary, metrics are the backbone of continuous improvement in DevOps. They provide the data needed to drive informed decisions, optimize processes, and ultimately deliver better software products and services to customers.

Section 13.5: Balancing Speed and Stability

In the world of DevOps, achieving a balance between speed and stability is a constant challenge. Organizations strive to deliver software quickly to meet market demands while ensuring that the software remains reliable and secure. This section explores the importance of striking this balance and provides strategies for doing so effectively.

The Need for Speed

Speed in software delivery has become a competitive advantage. Organizations that can release features, fixes, and updates rapidly can respond to customer needs more effectively and stay ahead of the competition. Speed is a fundamental tenet of DevOps, and it encompasses several key aspects:

1. Continuous Integration and Deployment (CI/CD):
Implementing CI/CD pipelines enables automated testing,
integration, and deployment, reducing manual intervention and

accelerating the release process.

2. Microservices and Containerization: These architectural approaches allow for more modular and scalable development, making it easier to develop, test, and deploy components independently.

3. Automation: Automating repetitive tasks, such as provisioning infrastructure or running tests, frees up valuable time and accelerates development and deployment.

4. Parallelization: Performing tasks in parallel, such as running tests concurrently, can significantly reduce lead times in the development pipeline.

The Importance of Stability

While speed is crucial, stability is equally important. Stability ensures that software behaves as expected, without unexpected crashes, security vulnerabilities, or performance issues. It's essential for maintaining customer trust and preventing costly downtime or data breaches. Key aspects of stability include:

1. Quality Assurance and Testing: Rigorous testing practices, including automated testing, security testing, and performance testing, are vital for ensuring software stability.

2. Security: Incorporating security practices throughout the development process (DevSecOps) helps identify and mitigate vulnerabilities before they reach production.

3. Monitoring and Observability: Real-time monitoring of applications and infrastructure allows for proactive issue identification and resolution, reducing downtime.

4. Incident Response: Having robust incident response processes in place ensures that when issues do arise, they are addressed promptly and efficiently.

Strategies for Balancing Speed and Stability

1. **Risk-Based Approach**: Assess the criticality of different parts of your software. Not all components require the same level of rigor in testing and deployment. Focus your efforts on high-impact areas.
2. **Release Trains**: Implement release trains or feature flags to decouple feature releases from deployments. This allows features to be developed and tested independently before being enabled.
3. **Automated Testing**: Invest in comprehensive automated testing to catch issues early in the development process. This reduces the risk of releasing unstable software.
4. **Environment Management**: Use infrastructure as code (IaC) and containerization to ensure consistency between development, testing, and production environments. This minimizes surprises during deployment.
5. **Continuous Monitoring**: Implement continuous monitoring and alerting to detect issues in real-time. Proactive issue identification allows for faster incident response.
6. **Collaboration**: Foster collaboration between development, operations, and security teams. Cross-functional collaboration ensures that stability is a shared responsibility.
7. **Feedback Loops**: Use feedback loops to continuously

assess the impact of changes on stability. This includes post-incident reviews and customer feedback.

8. **Performance Optimization**: Regularly optimize the performance of your software to prevent degradation over time. This includes addressing technical debt and code refactoring.

In conclusion, DevOps organizations must find the right balance between speed and stability to succeed in today's competitive landscape. Speed without stability can lead to unreliable software, while stability without speed can result in missed opportunities. Achieving this balance requires a combination of automated practices, rigorous testing, and a culture of collaboration and continuous improvement.

Chapter 14: The Role of Artificial Intelligence in DevOps

Section 14.1: AI-Driven DevOps: An Overview

Artificial Intelligence (AI) has rapidly evolved and is making significant inroads into various industries, including software development and operations. In the context of DevOps, AI is becoming a game-changer by enabling automation, predictive analytics, and data-driven decision-making. This section provides an overview of AI's role in DevOps and its potential to revolutionize the way organizations deliver software.

The Marriage of AI and DevOps

DevOps, with its emphasis on automation, collaboration, and continuous improvement, aligns seamlessly with AI's capabilities. AI-driven DevOps, often referred to as "AIOps," leverages AI and machine learning to enhance several aspects of the DevOps lifecycle:

1. Automation: AI can automate routine, time-consuming tasks across the development pipeline, from code testing and deployment to infrastructure provisioning. This reduces human error, speeds up processes, and enables quicker software releases.

2. Predictive Analytics: AI analyzes vast amounts of data generated during development and operations, identifying patterns and anomalies. It can predict potential issues, such as performance bottlenecks or security vulnerabilities, before they impact users.

3. Root Cause Analysis: When incidents occur, AI can perform root cause analysis faster and more accurately than manual investigation. It traces issues back to their source, helping teams resolve problems promptly.

4. Optimization: AI continuously optimizes infrastructure and application performance. It can scale resources based on real-time demand, ensuring optimal user experiences and cost efficiency.

5. Security: AI enhances security by detecting and responding to threats in real time. It can analyze user behavior, identify unusual patterns, and block malicious activity, reducing the risk of data breaches.

Use Cases of AI in DevOps

AI's impact on DevOps is far-reaching and extends across various use cases:

1. Automated Testing: AI-powered testing tools can generate test cases, execute tests, and identify defects, reducing the manual effort required for testing.

2. Continuous Monitoring: AI monitors application and infrastructure performance 24/7, providing instant alerts when issues arise. It also offers insights into historical performance data.

3. Anomaly Detection: AI can spot unusual patterns in log data, flagging potential security threats or performance anomalies that might otherwise go unnoticed.

4. Release Management: AI helps optimize release schedules, taking into account factors like code quality, test coverage, and user feedback.

5. Chatbots and Virtual Assistants: AI-driven chatbots can assist teams by providing instant answers to common queries, reducing response times, and improving collaboration.

6. Infrastructure Management: AI automates tasks such as provisioning, scaling, and load balancing, ensuring efficient resource utilization.

Implementing AI-Driven DevOps

Implementing AI in DevOps requires careful planning and consideration. Here are some steps to get started:

1. **Identify Use Cases**: Determine which aspects of your DevOps pipeline can benefit most from AI. Focus on areas that can deliver the most significant impact, such as automated testing or continuous monitoring.

2. **Data Collection**: Collect relevant data from your development and operational processes. This data will serve as the foundation for AI-driven insights and predictions.

3. **Choose the Right Tools**: Select AI tools and platforms that align with your organization's needs and goals. Consider factors like scalability, ease of integration, and vendor support.

4. **Training and Integration**: Train AI models using historical data, and integrate them into your DevOps processes. Ensure that AI systems work seamlessly with your existing tools and workflows.

5. **Monitoring and Fine-Tuning**: Continuously monitor AI performance and fine-tune models to improve accuracy. AI models should adapt to evolving software and infrastructure changes.

6. **Security and Compliance**: Pay close attention to security when implementing AI in DevOps. Ensure that AI systems are protected against attacks and adhere to relevant compliance standards.

7. **Cultural Shift**: Foster a culture of AI adoption and data-driven decision-making within your DevOps teams. Encourage collaboration between data scientists, developers, and operations personnel.

In conclusion, AI is revolutionizing DevOps by automating tasks, providing predictive insights, and enhancing overall efficiency. Organizations that embrace AI-driven DevOps are better positioned to deliver high-quality software faster, respond to issues proactively, and stay competitive in the rapidly evolving tech landscape.

Section 14.2: Machine Learning for Predictive Analytics in DevOps

In the realm of DevOps, predictive analytics powered by machine learning is a game-changer. It enables organizations to anticipate and mitigate issues, optimize resources, and streamline their software development and delivery pipelines. This section delves into the role of machine learning in predictive analytics within the DevOps ecosystem.

The Power of Predictive Analytics

Predictive analytics involves using historical data and machine learning algorithms to forecast future trends, identify potential issues, and make informed decisions. In DevOps, predictive analytics is leveraged in several key areas:

1. Predicting Performance Issues: Machine learning models can analyze past performance data and predict when applications or infrastructure might experience bottlenecks or degradation. This enables proactive optimization.

2. Preventing Downtime: By monitoring system logs and metrics in real-time, machine learning algorithms can detect anomalies that may lead to system failures. Predictive analytics helps prevent unplanned downtime.

3. Optimizing Resource Allocation: Predictive models can forecast resource requirements based on historical usage patterns. This ensures that resources are allocated efficiently, reducing costs and optimizing performance.

4. Quality Assurance: Machine learning can predict which parts of the codebase are more likely to contain defects. This guides testing efforts, allowing teams to focus on high-risk areas.

5. Release Planning: Predictive analytics assists in release planning by estimating the stability and quality of software builds. It helps teams decide when a build is ready for deployment.

6. Security Threat Detection: Predictive models can identify unusual patterns in system behavior that might indicate security threats. Early detection is crucial for minimizing security risks.

Implementing Machine Learning for Predictive Analytics

Implementing machine learning for predictive analytics in DevOps involves several key steps:

1. **Data Collection**: Start by collecting relevant historical data from your DevOps pipeline, including metrics, logs, and performance data. Ensure data quality and consistency.
2. **Data Preparation**: Clean, preprocess, and transform the data to make it suitable for machine learning algorithms. Feature engineering may be necessary to create meaningful input features.
3. **Model Selection**: Choose machine learning algorithms that are suitable for your predictive analytics use cases. Common algorithms include regression, classification, time series forecasting, and anomaly detection.
4. **Training**: Train your machine learning models using historical data. Use a portion of the data for training and another portion for validation to assess model performance.
5. **Integration**: Integrate the trained models into your

DevOps processes. This may involve connecting them to monitoring systems, alerting mechanisms, or release pipelines.

6. **Monitoring and Retraining**: Continuously monitor model performance in production. Models may degrade over time due to changes in the environment. Retrain models with fresh data as needed.

7. **Collaboration**: Encourage collaboration between data scientists, DevOps engineers, and other relevant teams. Clear communication is crucial for successful implementation.

Tools and Platforms

Several tools and platforms facilitate the integration of machine learning into DevOps processes:

- **Jupyter Notebook**: Jupyter notebooks are popular for data exploration, model development, and documentation.

- **TensorFlow and PyTorch**: These deep learning frameworks provide libraries and tools for building and deploying machine learning models.

- **Kubeflow**: Kubeflow is designed for deploying machine learning workflows on Kubernetes, making it easier to manage models in production.

- **Prometheus and Grafana**: These monitoring and visualization tools can be extended with machine learning capabilities to enhance observability.

- **Cloud-based AI Services**: Cloud providers offer machine learning services that can be integrated into DevOps pipelines, simplifying the deployment of AI models.

In conclusion, machine learning for predictive analytics has a transformative impact on DevOps by enhancing efficiency, reliability, and security. Organizations that harness the power of machine learning can proactively address issues, reduce downtime, and optimize resource allocation, ultimately delivering higher-quality software to their users.

Section 14.3: Automating DevOps Tasks with AI

Artificial Intelligence (AI) is revolutionizing the DevOps landscape by automating tasks, improving efficiency, and enhancing decision-making. In this section, we explore how AI is used to automate various aspects of DevOps processes.

The Role of AI in DevOps Automation

AI-driven automation in DevOps is a game-changer. It helps organizations streamline their software development, testing, deployment, and monitoring processes. Here are some key areas where AI plays a pivotal role:

1. Continuous Integration and Continuous Deployment (CI/CD):

- *Code Analysis*: AI-driven code analysis tools can automatically identify coding issues, security vulnerabilities, and code smells. This ensures that only high-quality code enters the CI/CD pipeline.

- *Test Automation*: AI-powered testing tools can generate and execute test cases automatically, significantly reducing the testing effort and time required.

- *Deployment Optimization*: AI algorithms can optimize deployment strategies, choosing the most suitable environments and configurations based on historical data and current conditions.

2. Predictive Maintenance:

- *Infrastructure Monitoring*: AI can monitor infrastructure in real-time and predict when components or servers are likely to fail. This enables proactive maintenance to prevent downtime.

- *Application Performance*: AI-driven analytics can predict application performance issues and bottlenecks, allowing for timely optimizations.

3. Security:

- *Threat Detection*: AI-based security tools can detect and respond to security threats in real-time by analyzing patterns and anomalies in system behavior.

- *Vulnerability Scanning*: AI automates vulnerability scanning by identifying weaknesses in software and infrastructure.

4. Resource Management:

- *Auto-scaling*: AI algorithms can automatically scale resources up or down based on demand, optimizing resource usage and reducing costs.

- *Resource Allocation*: AI helps allocate resources efficiently, ensuring that applications have the necessary computing power and storage.

5. Release Management:

- *Risk Assessment*: AI assesses the risk associated with software releases by analyzing code quality, test coverage, and historical data. This informs decisions about when to release new features or updates.

- *Deployment Decisions*: AI can automate deployment decisions by considering factors like user traffic, application stability, and performance.

Implementing AI Automation in DevOps

Implementing AI-driven automation in DevOps requires a well-defined strategy and the right tools. Here are the key steps:

1. **Identify Use Cases**: Determine which DevOps processes can benefit most from AI automation. Prioritize use cases based on their potential impact on efficiency and reliability.
2. **Data Collection**: Collect and store relevant data, including historical performance metrics, logs, and code repositories. High-quality data is essential for training AI

models.

3. **Model Selection**: Choose AI models and algorithms that align with your use cases. Common choices include machine learning, deep learning, and natural language processing models.

4. **Training and Validation**: Train AI models using historical data and validate their performance. Ensure that models generalize well to real-world scenarios.

5. **Integration**: Integrate AI models into your DevOps pipeline, monitoring systems, and other relevant tools. Ensure seamless communication between AI components and existing processes.

6. **Monitoring and Maintenance**: Continuously monitor the performance of AI-driven automation. Update models as needed to adapt to changing conditions and requirements.

7. **Collaboration**: Foster collaboration between data scientists, AI experts, and DevOps teams. Effective communication is crucial for successful implementation.

Tools and Platforms

Several tools and platforms facilitate the integration of AI automation into DevOps:

- **Machine Learning Frameworks**: Frameworks like TensorFlow, PyTorch, and scikit-learn provide libraries and tools for building AI models.

- **Automation Tools**: DevOps automation platforms like Jenkins, Ansible, and Puppet can be extended with AI capabilities.

- **AI-Driven Monitoring**: Tools like Prometheus and Grafana can leverage AI to enhance real-time monitoring and alerting.

- **Cloud-based AI Services**: Cloud providers offer AI services that can be integrated into DevOps workflows, simplifying AI model deployment.

In conclusion, AI-driven automation is reshaping DevOps by optimizing processes, improving reliability, and enhancing security. Organizations that embrace AI automation gain a competitive edge by delivering higher-quality software faster and with reduced operational overhead. As AI continues to advance, its role in DevOps automation will become even more critical for innovation and success.

Section 14.4: AI in Continuous Testing

Continuous Testing is an essential component of the DevOps pipeline, ensuring that software is thoroughly tested throughout the development lifecycle. Artificial Intelligence (AI) is revolutionizing Continuous Testing by making it faster, more efficient, and capable of identifying complex issues that may be missed by traditional testing methods.

The Role of AI in Continuous Testing

AI enhances Continuous Testing in various ways:

1. *Test Automation:*

- *Test Script Generation*: AI can automatically generate test scripts based on application behavior, reducing the manual effort required for test case creation.

- *Self-healing Tests*: AI can identify and fix flaky or failing tests by analyzing patterns and historical test data, improving test reliability.

2. *Test Execution:*

- *Parallel Testing*: AI enables parallel test execution across multiple environments and configurations, significantly reducing test execution time.

- *Test Prioritization*: AI algorithms prioritize tests based on code changes and potential impact, ensuring that critical tests run first.

3. *Test Data Management:*

- *Data Generation*: AI generates synthetic test data, ensuring that test cases cover a wide range of scenarios without exposing sensitive information.

- *Data Masking*: AI can mask or anonymize sensitive data in test environments to comply with privacy regulations.

4. Defect Detection:

- *Anomaly Detection*: AI identifies anomalies in application behavior, helping detect defects that might otherwise go unnoticed.

- *Log Analysis*: AI analyzes logs and error messages to pinpoint issues quickly, reducing debugging time.

5. Performance Testing:

- *Load Testing*: AI simulates user behavior and traffic patterns to perform realistic load testing, helping teams identify performance bottlenecks.

- *Scalability Testing*: AI-driven tests assess an application's scalability under different conditions.

6. Regression Testing:

- *Change Impact Analysis*: AI analyzes code changes and predicts which areas of the application are likely to be affected, allowing targeted regression testing.

- *Automated Regression Suites*: AI updates regression test suites automatically when code changes occur.

Implementing AI in Continuous Testing

Integrating AI into Continuous Testing requires a systematic approach:

1. **Identify Use Cases**: Determine where AI can bring the

most value in your testing processes. Focus on areas with repetitive tasks, high complexity, or a need for rapid feedback.

2. **Data Collection**: Gather historical testing data, including test cases, logs, and performance metrics. High-quality data is essential for training AI models.

3. **Model Selection**: Choose appropriate AI models, such as machine learning classifiers for defect detection or reinforcement learning for test optimization.

4. **Training and Validation**: Train AI models using labeled data and validate their performance against a hold-out dataset. Continuously refine models for better accuracy.

5. **Integration**: Embed AI-driven testing components into your Continuous Testing pipeline. Ensure seamless communication with existing tools and processes.

6. **Feedback Loop**: Establish a feedback loop to continuously improve AI models. Monitor their performance and update them as necessary.

Tools and Platforms

Several tools and platforms can assist in implementing AI in Continuous Testing:

- **Test Automation Frameworks**: Frameworks like Selenium, Appium, and TestNG can be extended with AI capabilities.

- **AI-Powered Testing Tools**: Tools like Applitools and Test.ai offer AI-driven visual testing and test case generation.

- **Performance Testing Tools**: AI-driven performance testing tools like LoadRunner can simulate realistic user behavior.

- **Test Management Systems**: Some test management systems integrate AI for test case management and execution.

In summary, AI is reshaping Continuous Testing by making it smarter, more efficient, and capable of detecting defects early in the development process. Organizations that adopt AI-driven Continuous Testing practices can release high-quality software faster, reduce testing costs, and improve overall product reliability. As AI technology continues to advance, its impact on Continuous Testing will become increasingly profound, contributing to the success of DevOps initiatives.

Section 14.5: Future Trends: AI and DevOps

Artificial Intelligence (AI) and DevOps, two rapidly evolving fields in the world of technology, are increasingly converging to drive innovation and efficiency in software development and operations. As we look to the future, several exciting trends and possibilities emerge at the intersection of AI and DevOps.

1. AI-Powered Automation

AI-driven automation will play a central role in DevOps processes. Machine learning algorithms will continuously analyze data from development, testing, and production environments to automate decision-making, such as code deployment, scaling, and resource allocation. This will lead to more efficient and self-optimizing DevOps pipelines.

2. Predictive Analytics

AI will be used to predict potential issues in the software development lifecycle. By analyzing historical data, AI models can forecast software defects, performance bottlenecks, and infrastructure failures. This proactive approach will help teams address problems before they impact users.

3. Self-Healing Systems

AI-powered systems will become adept at self-diagnosis and self-correction. When anomalies are detected, AI will automatically trigger remediation actions, such as rolling back changes, adjusting resource allocation, or scaling the infrastructure to maintain system health.

4. Natural Language Processing (NLP)

NLP-powered chatbots and virtual assistants will assist DevOps teams in tasks like troubleshooting, incident response, and providing real-time information. This enhances communication and collaboration within DevOps teams and across the organization.

5. AI-Enhanced Testing

AI will continue to revolutionize software testing. Automated test case generation, self-learning testing scripts, and AI-driven test data generation will become standard practices, reducing manual testing efforts and improving test coverage.

6. Security and Compliance

AI will play a pivotal role in enhancing security in DevOps, known as DevSecOps. AI algorithms will continuously monitor for security vulnerabilities, detect unusual behavior, and enforce compliance with security standards. This proactive approach will minimize security risks.

7. Explainable AI (XAI)

As AI systems become more integrated into DevOps, there will be a growing need for XAI. DevOps professionals will require transparency into AI decision-making processes, especially in critical areas like automated deployments and incident management.

8. AI-Driven DataOps

DataOps, a practice that focuses on improving the flow of data in the DevOps pipeline, will leverage AI for data quality assessment, data transformation, and data lineage tracking. AI will ensure that data-driven applications are reliable and performant.

9. Ethical AI Practices

As AI becomes deeply ingrained in DevOps, ethical considerations will be paramount. DevOps teams will need to establish guidelines and practices to ensure that AI is used responsibly, without bias, and in compliance with privacy and data protection regulations.

10. AI for Resource Optimization

AI will help optimize resource allocation in cloud and on-premises environments. AI-driven algorithms will dynamically adjust infrastructure resources based on application demand, optimizing costs and performance.

11. AI-Driven Observability

AI-powered observability tools will provide real-time insights into application and infrastructure health. These tools will automatically correlate data from multiple sources and identify root causes of issues, reducing mean time to resolution.

12. AI for Code Quality

AI will assist in maintaining high code quality standards by automatically reviewing code for adherence to coding standards, identifying potential vulnerabilities, and suggesting improvements.

13. AI in Release Management

AI will aid in intelligent release management by predicting the impact of code changes and recommending safe deployment windows. This will reduce the risk of deployment failures.

In conclusion, the integration of AI and DevOps is an exciting frontier that promises to enhance software development and operations in numerous ways. As organizations increasingly adopt AI technologies, staying informed about these future trends and their potential applications will be crucial for staying competitive in the rapidly evolving technology landscape. The synergy between AI and DevOps will continue to drive innovation, efficiency, and reliability in software development and delivery.

Chapter 15: Managing Dependencies and Version Control

Section 15.1: Understanding Dependency Management in DevOps

Dependency management is a critical aspect of DevOps, ensuring that software projects are built and run efficiently with all the necessary components and libraries. In this section, we'll delve into the fundamentals of dependency management in the context of DevOps and explore the key concepts, challenges, and best practices associated with it.

What Are Dependencies?

Dependencies in software development refer to external components, libraries, or modules that a project relies on to function correctly. These can include third-party libraries, frameworks, packages, or even other internal modules within the same project. Dependencies are an integral part of modern software development, enabling developers to leverage existing code and avoid reinventing the wheel.

The Importance of Dependency Management

Effective dependency management is crucial for several reasons:

1. **Ensuring Reproducibility:** Dependency management ensures that a project's build and runtime environments are reproducible. This means that regardless of when or where a project is built or deployed, it will use the same set of dependencies, reducing the chances of compatibility issues.
2. **Security:** Managing dependencies allows for the

identification and mitigation of security vulnerabilities.
Regularly updating dependencies to their latest secure
versions helps protect the software from known exploits.

3. **Efficiency:** Proper management helps reduce the size of
deployment packages, improving efficiency in terms of
storage, bandwidth, and deployment times.

4. **Stability:** Dependency management ensures that a
project's dependencies are stable and reliable. Unstable or
deprecated dependencies can lead to unexpected issues and
downtime.

Challenges in Dependency Management

While dependency management offers many benefits, it comes with
its own set of challenges:

1. **Version Compatibility:** Ensuring that different
dependencies work together seamlessly can be complex,
especially when multiple dependencies have conflicting
version requirements.

2. **Dependency Hell:** Managing a large number of
dependencies, each with its own set of dependencies, can
become overwhelming and lead to what's known as
"dependency hell." This situation makes it difficult to track
and resolve conflicts.

3. **Security Risks:** Ignoring updates to dependencies can
introduce security risks, as outdated versions may have
known vulnerabilities.

4. **License Compliance:** Many dependencies come with
specific licenses that must be adhered to. Ensuring
compliance with these licenses is essential to avoid legal
issues.

Best Practices for Dependency Management

To effectively manage dependencies in DevOps, consider the following best practices:

1. **Dependency Files:** Use dependency files or manifests (e.g., package.json, requirements.txt, Gemfile) to declare project dependencies explicitly. These files serve as documentation and automation tools for dependency management.

2. **Version Pinning:** Pin dependencies to specific versions or version ranges to control updates and ensure stability. Avoid overly broad version constraints that may lead to compatibility issues.

3. **Dependency Resolution:** Utilize dependency resolution tools to automatically resolve and fetch dependencies, reducing manual effort.

4. **Dependency Scanning:** Regularly scan dependencies for known security vulnerabilities using automated tools. Integrate this process into your CI/CD pipeline to catch issues early.

5. **Testing:** Include dependency updates in your automated testing process to identify any breaking changes or regressions caused by updates.

6. **Automation:** Automate dependency management tasks, including updates and vulnerability checks, to ensure consistency and reduce manual intervention.

7. **Documentation:** Maintain clear and up-to-date documentation regarding dependencies, including licensing information and reasons for choosing specific versions.

8. **Regular Updates:** Stay proactive by regularly updating dependencies to their latest secure versions, while ensuring

compatibility and conducting thorough testing.

9. **Fallback Plans:** Have contingency plans in place for handling unexpected issues, such as rolling back to a previous version or applying patches.

Effective dependency management is a critical part of DevOps, contributing to the reliability, security, and maintainability of software projects. By following best practices and staying vigilant, DevOps teams can navigate the complex landscape of dependencies successfully, ultimately delivering more robust and secure software.

Section 15.2: Version Control Systems and Strategies

Version control is a fundamental component of modern software development and an integral part of managing dependencies in DevOps. In this section, we'll explore version control systems (VCS) and strategies that enable teams to effectively manage their codebase, track changes, collaborate seamlessly, and maintain a history of project revisions.

Version Control Systems (VCS)

Version control systems, also known as source code management systems, are tools that help developers track changes to their codebase over time. They provide a structured way to manage and collaborate on code, ensuring that multiple developers can work on the same project without conflicts. Here are some commonly used version control systems:

1. **Git:** Git is the most widely used distributed version control system. It allows developers to track changes, work on branches, and merge code easily. Git is known for its

speed and flexibility, making it a popular choice for projects of all sizes.

2. **Subversion (SVN):** SVN is a centralized version control system that stores code on a central server. It offers robust access control and is suitable for projects that require strict security and centralized management.

3. **Mercurial:** Mercurial is another distributed version control system that focuses on simplicity and ease of use. It provides a similar feature set to Git and is often chosen for its user-friendly interface.

4. **Perforce (Helix Core):** Perforce is a centralized version control system designed for large enterprises and industries that require strict compliance and auditing. It is known for its scalability and performance.

Key Concepts in Version Control

To understand version control, you need to grasp some key concepts:

1. **Repository:** A repository, or repo, is a central storage location for all project files and their complete history. It's where all code versions and changes are stored.

2. **Commit:** A commit is a snapshot of changes made to the codebase at a specific point in time. Commits are accompanied by commit messages that describe the purpose of the changes.

3. **Branch:** A branch is a separate line of development that allows developers to work on new features or bug fixes without affecting the main codebase. Branches are created from the main codebase and can be merged back when the changes are complete.

4. **Merge:** Merging is the process of integrating changes from

one branch into another. This is how multiple developers collaborate and ensure their work is combined into the main codebase.

5. **Pull Request (PR) or Merge Request (MR):** A pull request (commonly used in Git) or merge request (commonly used in GitLab) is a request to merge changes from one branch into another. It includes code review and discussion before the changes are merged.

Version Control Strategies

Effective version control strategies are essential for managing dependencies and code changes in a DevOps environment. Here are some strategies commonly used by DevOps teams:

1. **Feature Branch Workflow:** Developers work on separate feature branches, making changes isolated from the main codebase. Once features are complete, they are merged back into the main branch.

2. **Gitflow Workflow:** A branching model that defines different branches for features, releases, and hotfixes. It provides a structured approach to code management.

3. **Trunk-Based Development:** Developers work directly on the main branch, reducing the complexity of managing multiple branches. Frequent small commits and continuous integration are key to this strategy.

4. **GitOps:** An approach that uses Git repositories as the source of truth for infrastructure and deployment configurations. Changes in Git trigger automated deployments, enabling Infrastructure as Code (IaC) practices.

5. **Versioned Dependencies:** Include version information for external dependencies in your code repository. This ensures

that the codebase uses specific, tested versions of libraries and frameworks.

6. **Continuous Integration:** Automatically build and test code changes whenever they are committed to the repository. CI pipelines help catch integration issues early.

7. **Automated Releases:** Automate the release process to ensure that new versions of your software are consistently built, tested, and deployed.

8. **Code Reviews:** Incorporate code reviews into your version control process to maintain code quality and consistency.

Version control is a cornerstone of modern software development and DevOps practices. Choosing the right version control system and implementing effective strategies can significantly improve collaboration, code quality, and the overall DevOps workflow.

Section 15.3: Handling Dependency Conflicts and Issues

In the world of software development, managing dependencies is a common challenge. Dependencies are external libraries, packages, or modules that your project relies on to function correctly. While dependencies bring numerous advantages, such as code reuse and accelerated development, they also introduce the risk of conflicts and issues. In this section, we will explore strategies for handling dependency conflicts and common problems that may arise.

Understanding Dependency Conflicts

Dependency conflicts occur when two or more components of your project depend on different versions of the same library or package. These conflicts can manifest in various ways:

1. **Compile-Time Conflicts:** These conflicts arise when there are conflicting types or interfaces between different versions of a library. The compiler may be unable to resolve which version to use, resulting in errors.
2. **Runtime Conflicts:** Runtime conflicts occur when a project runs successfully but encounters issues during execution. These issues may include unexpected behavior, crashes, or incorrect results due to incompatible library versions.
3. **Transitive Dependencies:** Many dependencies rely on other libraries, known as transitive dependencies. When different parts of your project depend on different versions of a transitive dependency, it can lead to conflicts.

Strategies for Handling Dependency Conflicts

1. **Dependency Locking:** Dependency locking tools like Yarn, npm's package-lock.json, or Rust's Cargo.lock record the exact versions of dependencies that have been tested and are known to work. This ensures that the same versions are used consistently across different environments.
2. **Semantic Versioning (SemVer):** Following Semantic Versioning guidelines helps mitigate conflicts by allowing developers to understand how changes to a library affect backward compatibility. Libraries following SemVer indicate whether changes are major, minor, or patch releases, making it easier to assess the impact of updates.
3. **Dependency Resolution Tools:** Dependency resolution tools like Maven in the Java ecosystem or Bundler in Ruby help manage dependencies by resolving conflicts and ensuring that compatible versions are used.
4. **Dependency Auditing:** Regularly audit your project's dependencies for security vulnerabilities and compatibility

issues. Tools like npm audit, pipenv check, or OWASP Dependency-Check can help identify potential problems.

5. **Dependency Isolation:** Use virtual environments or containers like Docker to isolate your project and its dependencies from other system libraries. This reduces the risk of conflicts with system-wide dependencies.

6. **Manual Dependency Selection:** In some cases, you may need to manually select specific versions of dependencies to resolve conflicts. Ensure that the selected versions are compatible with your project's requirements.

7. **Testing and Continuous Integration:** Implement robust testing and continuous integration (CI) pipelines that check for dependency conflicts as part of your development workflow. CI tools can alert you to issues early in the development process.

Common Dependency Issues and Solutions

1. **Circular Dependencies:** Circular dependencies occur when two or more components depend on each other. To resolve them, refactor your code to break the circular relationship or use interfaces and abstractions to decouple the dependencies.

2. **Outdated Dependencies:** Regularly update your dependencies to the latest versions to benefit from bug fixes, new features, and security patches. However, be cautious and test thoroughly after updates to avoid introducing new issues.

3. **Unmaintained Dependencies:** Sometimes, dependencies become unmaintained or obsolete. In such cases, consider finding alternative libraries or, if feasible, maintaining the dependency yourself.

4. **License Compatibility:** Ensure that the licenses of your

project's dependencies are compatible with your project's licensing requirements. Some licenses may introduce legal conflicts.

Handling dependency conflicts and issues is an ongoing aspect of software development. By adopting best practices, using dependency management tools, and staying vigilant, you can reduce the likelihood of conflicts and ensure a smooth development process.

Section 15.4: Automating Dependency Updates

Automating the process of updating dependencies is a crucial practice in modern software development. Keeping your project's dependencies up-to-date is essential for security, stability, and the ability to leverage the latest features and improvements from the software ecosystem. In this section, we will explore strategies and tools for automating dependency updates effectively.

Manual vs. Automated Updates

Manually updating dependencies can be a time-consuming and error-prone process. Developers need to regularly check for updates, understand the changes, and then apply the updates cautiously to avoid introducing breaking changes or conflicts. Automated updates offer several advantages:

1. **Efficiency:** Automation tools can monitor dependencies continuously and notify you when updates are available. This eliminates the need for manual tracking and reduces the time spent on updates.
2. **Consistency:** Automated updates ensure that all team members use the same dependency versions, reducing the

risk of conflicts and discrepancies in development environments.

3. **Security:** Automated tools can quickly detect and address security vulnerabilities by updating to patched versions of libraries or packages.

4. **Easier Rollbacks:** Automated updates often include version locking mechanisms, making it easier to roll back to a previous version in case of issues.

Strategies for Automated Dependency Updates

1. **Dependency Management Tools:** Many package managers provide built-in or third-party tools for automating dependency updates. For example, npm offers npm-check-updates and npm-check, while Python has pip-tools and pyup.

2. **Continuous Integration (CI):** Incorporate automated dependency checks and updates into your CI/CD pipeline. CI services like Travis CI, CircleCI, or GitHub Actions can run update scripts when changes to dependencies are detected.

3. **Dependency Update Services:** Consider using dedicated dependency update services like Dependabot (now part of GitHub) or Renovate. These services automatically create pull requests to update dependencies when new versions are available.

4. **Semantic Versioning (SemVer):** Configure your automated update tools to follow Semantic Versioning guidelines. This ensures that updates are categorized correctly as major, minor, or patch releases, helping you understand the potential impact of each update.

5. **Scheduled Updates:** Establish a regular schedule for automated updates. For example, you can set up weekly or

monthly checks for dependency updates to ensure that you stay current with the latest changes.

6. **Testing and Monitoring:** After automated updates, run your test suite to ensure that the new dependency versions do not introduce regressions. Implement monitoring to detect any unusual behavior in your application after updates.

7. **Version Pinning:** While automated updates are valuable, it's essential to maintain control over your project's dependencies. Use version pinning to specify the acceptable version ranges for each dependency to prevent unexpected major updates.

Example Automation Workflow

Here's a simplified example of an automated dependency update workflow using GitHub Actions and the Dependabot service:

1. **GitHub Actions Setup:** Configure a GitHub Actions workflow that runs on a schedule or when changes to the project's package.json or requirements.txt files are detected.

2. **Dependabot Configuration:** Set up Dependabot with a configuration file that defines update policies and version constraints for your dependencies.

3. **Automated Pull Requests:** When Dependabot detects updates, it automatically creates pull requests in your GitHub repository. These pull requests include changes to your dependency files.

4. **Testing and Review:** GitHub Actions triggers the workflow, which builds and tests the project with the updated dependencies. Developers review the pull requests, and automated tests help identify any issues introduced by the updates.

5. **Merge or Rollback:** After review and testing, you can choose to merge the pull requests to accept the updates or roll back to the previous dependency versions if problems are detected.

Automating dependency updates is a proactive approach to maintaining your software project's health and security. By adopting automated tools and best practices, you can ensure that your dependencies remain current, secure, and compatible with your project's evolving requirements.

Section 15.5: Best Practices for Version Control in DevOps

Version control plays a central role in DevOps, enabling teams to collaborate effectively, track changes, and maintain a history of the project's evolution. In this section, we'll explore best practices for version control in the context of DevOps, emphasizing the importance of code repositories, branching strategies, and code review processes.

Use a Version Control System (VCS)

1. **Choose the Right VCS:** Select a version control system that aligns with your project's needs. Git is the most popular choice, providing distributed version control and robust collaboration features.
2. **Central Repository:** Establish a central repository as the source of truth for your project's codebase. Hosting services like GitHub, GitLab, and Bitbucket offer reliable options for hosting Git repositories.
3. **Version Everything:** Track not only your application code but also configuration files, scripts, and documentation.

Versioning everything ensures that your infrastructure and code changes are synchronized.

Branching Strategies

1. **Git Flow:** Adopt a branching model like Git Flow, which defines branch naming conventions and workflows for features, releases, hotfixes, and more. This structure helps manage development phases effectively.
2. **Feature Branches:** Create feature branches for new development work. Each feature branch should have a clear purpose and a corresponding issue or user story.
3. **Pull Requests (PRs):** Encourage the use of pull requests or merge requests for code review. PRs provide a structured way to propose and discuss changes before merging them into the main branch.
4. **Branch Permissions:** Implement branch permissions to control who can merge changes into specific branches. Limit direct pushes to critical branches to reduce the risk of accidental or unauthorized changes.

Code Review

1. **Code Review Process:** Establish a code review process that includes reviewing code for quality, correctness, and adherence to coding standards. Use code review tools like GitHub's or GitLab's built-in review features.
2. **Automated Checks:** Integrate automated code analysis tools and linters into your CI/CD pipeline. These tools can catch common issues and enforce coding standards before code is even reviewed.
3. **Reviewer Rotation:** Rotate code reviewers to distribute knowledge and avoid bottlenecks. Encourage constructive

feedback and collaboration during reviews.

4. **Feedback and Documentation:** Provide clear feedback during code reviews and ensure that changes are documented, including the rationale for decisions made during the review.

Continuous Integration and Version Control

1. **CI/CD Integration:** Integrate your version control system with your CI/CD pipeline. Trigger builds, tests, and deployments automatically upon code changes.
2. **Artifact Management:** Use a package manager or artifact repository to store and version artifacts produced during the build process. This ensures reproducibility and traceability.

Branch Cleanup

1. **Prune Stale Branches:** Regularly review and remove stale or obsolete branches. Consider automating this process to keep your repository clean.
2. **Archiving Releases:** After a release is completed, consider archiving the associated branch to preserve its state while reducing clutter in the active branches.

Documentation

1. **Versioning Documentation:** Keep documentation in sync with code changes by versioning it along with the codebase. Use tools like Markdown or reStructuredText for easy integration with VCS.
2. **README Files:** Maintain clear and up-to-date README files in repositories to provide essential

information about the project's purpose, setup, and usage.

Security and Access Control

1. **Access Control:** Enforce access control to restrict who can modify code and configuration files. Ensure that permissions are appropriately configured to prevent unauthorized changes.
2. **Secret Management:** Safeguard sensitive information such as API keys, passwords, and encryption keys. Use secret management tools to store secrets securely and avoid hardcoding them in code.

Compliance and Auditing

1. **Audit Trails:** Enable auditing and logging features in your VCS and CI/CD systems. Maintain audit trails to track changes and user activities for compliance and security purposes.
2. **Compliance Standards:** Depending on your industry or project requirements, adhere to specific compliance standards such as GDPR, HIPAA, or PCI DSS by implementing version control practices that support compliance.

Following these best practices for version control in DevOps helps ensure code quality, collaboration efficiency, and the ability to trace changes throughout the software development lifecycle. By integrating version control seamlessly into your DevOps processes, you can achieve greater visibility, traceability, and reliability in your software projects.

Chapter 16: Overcoming Common DevOps

Challenges

Section 16.1: Addressing Toolchain Complexity

In the ever-evolving landscape of DevOps, organizations face a multitude of challenges as they strive to streamline their software development and delivery processes. One of the most pervasive challenges is addressing toolchain complexity. DevOps toolchains encompass a wide array of tools that cover various stages of the software development lifecycle, from source code management to deployment and monitoring. While these tools are essential for automating tasks and ensuring a smooth flow of work, managing them can become a complex endeavor.

The Growing Toolchain Ecosystem

DevOps toolchains typically consist of version control systems (e.g., Git), continuous integration servers (e.g., Jenkins), containerization platforms (e.g., Docker), orchestration tools (e.g., Kubernetes), monitoring solutions (e.g., Prometheus), and many more. With the constant introduction of new tools and updates to existing ones, organizations often find themselves in a situation where they must choose and integrate tools wisely.

Challenges of Tool Selection

Selecting the right tools for a DevOps toolchain can be daunting. It involves considering factors such as compatibility with existing systems, scalability, ease of use, and the specific needs of your organization. Failing to choose the right tools can lead to inefficiencies and bottlenecks in the DevOps pipeline.

Integration and Interoperability

Once tools are selected, the next challenge is integrating them seamlessly. Many tools are designed to work together, but ensuring their interoperability can still be a complex task. Integration issues can lead to data silos, where information does not flow freely between tools, hindering collaboration and visibility across the DevOps process.

Managing Toolchain Complexity

To address toolchain complexity, organizations should adopt a strategic approach. Here are some best practices to consider:

1. **Assessment and Optimization:** Regularly assess your toolchain to identify redundancies and obsolete tools. Optimize your toolset to ensure you are using the most efficient options.
2. **Standardization:** Establish standards and guidelines for tool usage within your organization. This helps maintain consistency and reduces the complexity of managing multiple tools.
3. **Automation:** Automate integration and deployment processes as much as possible. Automation reduces the chances of manual errors and makes it easier to manage a diverse toolchain.
4. **Training and Documentation:** Ensure that your team is well-trained in using the tools. Provide comprehensive documentation to facilitate onboarding and troubleshooting.
5. **Monitoring and Analytics:** Implement monitoring and analytics solutions to gain insights into toolchain

performance. This helps in identifying bottlenecks and areas that require improvement.

6. **Regular Updates:** Keep your tools and integrations up to date. Staying current with the latest versions can provide access to new features and improvements.

7. **Feedback Loops:** Establish feedback loops within your organization to gather input from teams using the tools. This feedback can guide continuous improvement efforts.

By addressing toolchain complexity proactively and implementing these best practices, organizations can streamline their DevOps processes and ensure that their toolsets support, rather than hinder, their goals of faster and more reliable software delivery.

Section 16.2: Managing Configuration Drift

In the realm of DevOps, configuration management plays a pivotal role in maintaining consistency and repeatability across environments. However, managing configuration drift is a common challenge that organizations face when dealing with complex infrastructures and frequent changes.

Understanding Configuration Drift

Configuration drift occurs when the actual configuration of a system or infrastructure diverges from its desired state, as defined in your infrastructure as code (IaC) templates or configuration management tools. This discrepancy can result from various factors, including manual changes, unauthorized modifications, or updates that were not correctly applied.

Configuration drift can manifest in different forms:

1. **Software Versions:** Over time, software versions may vary

across servers or nodes, leading to inconsistencies and potential compatibility issues.

2. **Configuration Files:** Manual changes to configuration files, such as altering settings or permissions, can introduce drift.

3. **Security Policies:** Drift can impact security policies, potentially exposing vulnerabilities if security configurations deviate from the defined baseline.

4. **Hardware Differences:** In heterogeneous environments, differences in hardware configurations can contribute to drift, affecting performance and reliability.

The Impact of Configuration Drift

Configuration drift can have serious consequences for a DevOps environment:

- **Increased Complexity:** Managing systems with configuration drift becomes more complex and challenging, as there is no longer a single source of truth for configurations.

- **Reduced Reliability:** Drift can lead to unpredictable behavior, system failures, and decreased reliability, making it difficult to maintain high availability.

- **Security Risks:** Security configurations that drift from the intended state can expose systems to vulnerabilities and threats.

- **Debugging and Troubleshooting:** Identifying the root cause of issues becomes more difficult when configurations have drifted, prolonging troubleshooting efforts.

Strategies for Managing Configuration Drift

To effectively address configuration drift, organizations should implement strategies and best practices:

1. **Automation:** Automate configuration management using tools like Ansible, Puppet, or Chef to enforce desired configurations consistently.
2. **Continuous Monitoring:** Implement real-time monitoring and alerting to detect configuration drift as soon as it occurs.
3. **Version Control:** Store configuration files and IaC templates in version control systems (e.g., Git) to track changes and roll back to previous configurations if needed.
4. **Immutable Infrastructure:** Consider adopting immutable infrastructure practices, where infrastructure components are replaced rather than modified when changes are required.
5. **Baseline Configuration:** Establish a baseline configuration that defines the desired state of systems and continuously compare actual configurations against this baseline.
6. **Regular Audits:** Conduct regular audits to identify and rectify configuration drift, ensuring that systems remain compliant.
7. **Documentation:** Maintain comprehensive documentation of configurations and changes to facilitate tracking and troubleshooting.
8. **Access Control:** Implement strict access controls to prevent unauthorized changes to configurations.

By implementing these strategies, organizations can effectively manage configuration drift, maintain consistency, enhance system reliability, and reduce the risks associated with configuration discrepancies in their DevOps environments.

Section 16.3: Ensuring High Availability and Reliability

In a DevOps environment, ensuring high availability (HA) and reliability is paramount, as system downtime and failures can have significant consequences, including financial losses and damage to reputation. High availability refers to the ability of a system or application to remain operational and accessible even in the face of failures, while reliability focuses on consistent and error-free performance over time.

The Importance of High Availability and Reliability

High availability and reliability are crucial for several reasons:

1. **Business Continuity:** Downtime can disrupt operations, resulting in financial losses. High availability ensures business continuity by minimizing downtime.
2. **User Experience:** Reliability leads to a positive user experience. Users expect applications and services to work consistently without disruptions.
3. **Data Integrity:** Reliable systems protect data integrity, preventing data corruption or loss during operations.
4. **Competitive Advantage:** Organizations with highly available and reliable systems gain a competitive advantage by delivering consistent and dependable services to customers.

Strategies for Achieving High Availability

1. **Redundancy:** Introduce redundancy at critical points in the infrastructure, such as load balancers, databases, and servers. Redundancy ensures that if one component fails, another can take over without service interruption.
2. **Load Balancing:** Use load balancers to distribute traffic across multiple servers or instances, preventing overload and improving responsiveness.
3. **Failover Mechanisms:** Implement automatic failover mechanisms that detect failures and switch to backup systems seamlessly.
4. **Scalability:** Design systems to scale horizontally by adding more resources or instances as demand increases. Scalability enhances both availability and reliability.
5. **Monitoring and Alerting:** Continuously monitor the health of systems and applications. Set up alerts to proactively identify issues and address them before they impact users.
6. **Regular Backups:** Perform regular data backups and test the restoration process to ensure data recovery in case of failures.
7. **Disaster Recovery Plans:** Develop disaster recovery plans that outline procedures for recovering from catastrophic failures or events.

Ensuring Reliability

1. **Automated Testing:** Implement automated testing, including unit tests, integration tests, and end-to-end tests, to detect and prevent software defects.
2. **Continuous Integration and Deployment (CI/CD):** Use CI/CD pipelines to automate the deployment process and

ensure consistent and reliable releases.

3. **Rollback Plans:** Prepare rollback plans to revert to a previous version in case of issues introduced during deployments.

4. **Configuration Management:** Manage configurations rigorously to prevent drift and ensure consistency.

5. **Performance Monitoring:** Continuously monitor system performance to identify and address performance bottlenecks and resource constraints.

6. **Security Practices:** Implement security best practices to protect systems from vulnerabilities and attacks that can compromise reliability.

7. **Documentation:** Maintain up-to-date documentation that includes system architecture, configurations, and troubleshooting procedures.

By prioritizing high availability and reliability in your DevOps practices, you can minimize disruptions, enhance the user experience, and build trust with customers, ultimately contributing to the success of your organization's software and services.

Section 16.4: Dealing with Legacy Systems in DevOps

Legacy systems, often characterized by outdated technologies and architectures, present unique challenges when implementing DevOps practices. While DevOps is typically associated with modern, agile development, organizations that rely on legacy systems can still benefit from its principles. This section explores strategies for integrating DevOps into environments with legacy systems.

The Challenge of Legacy Systems

Legacy systems come with several challenges that make DevOps adoption more complex:

1. **Outdated Technology:** Legacy systems may run on obsolete technologies, making it difficult to implement modern CI/CD pipelines and automation.
2. **Lack of Documentation:** Older systems often lack comprehensive documentation, making it challenging to understand their architecture and dependencies.
3. **Resistance to Change:** Teams working with legacy systems may be resistant to adopting DevOps practices due to established processes and fear of disrupting stability.

Strategies for DevOps with Legacy Systems

1. **Assessment and Documentation:** Begin by conducting a thorough assessment of your legacy systems. Document their architecture, dependencies, and workflows. This documentation will be crucial for making informed decisions.
2. **Incremental Improvements:** Instead of attempting a complete overhaul, focus on making incremental improvements to legacy systems. Identify bottlenecks and pain points that can be addressed with DevOps practices.
3. **Isolate Legacy Components:** Consider isolating legacy components from the rest of your infrastructure. This allows you to apply DevOps practices to new components while maintaining the stability of the legacy systems.
4. **Wrapper Services:** Create wrapper services around legacy components to expose them as APIs. This enables integration with modern CI/CD pipelines and tools.

5. **Version Control:** Implement version control for configurations and scripts related to legacy systems. This helps manage changes and ensures consistency.

6. **Test Automation:** Gradually introduce automated testing for legacy components. Start with unit tests and expand to integration and regression testing.

7. **Continuous Monitoring:** Implement continuous monitoring to gain insights into the performance and behavior of legacy systems. Use this data to identify areas for improvement.

8. **Cultural Shift:** Foster a culture of collaboration and openness among teams working on legacy and modern systems. Encourage knowledge sharing and cross-training.

9. **Retire When Possible:** Identify legacy systems that are no longer critical to your organization's operations and consider retiring them in favor of modern alternatives.

Case Studies: Successful DevOps with Legacy Systems

Several organizations have successfully integrated DevOps practices with legacy systems:

- **US Federal Aviation Administration (FAA):** The FAA modernized its air traffic control systems while maintaining legacy systems' stability. They used wrapper services to expose legacy components as APIs and gradually introduced automation.

- **Healthcare Providers:** Many healthcare providers manage patient data on legacy systems. They adopted DevOps to improve data security, automate processes, and enhance patient care.

- **Financial Institutions:** Banks and financial institutions with mainframe systems have embraced DevOps to accelerate development and ensure compliance while managing legacy platforms.

In conclusion, integrating DevOps practices with legacy systems is challenging but achievable. By taking a strategic and incremental approach, organizations can modernize their processes and deliver value while preserving the stability of critical legacy systems.

Section 16.5: Lessons Learned from DevOps Failures

While DevOps has become a widely adopted approach for software development and operations, not all organizations have successful implementations. In this section, we'll explore common reasons behind DevOps failures and the lessons that can be learned from these experiences.

Common Causes of DevOps Failures

1. **Lack of Clear Goals:** One of the most common reasons for DevOps failures is the absence of clear and measurable goals. Organizations often adopt DevOps because it's trendy rather than aligning it with their specific needs.
2. **Resistance to Change:** DevOps requires a cultural shift, and resistance to change from teams and individuals can hinder progress. People may be attached to existing processes and technologies.
3. **Inadequate Training:** Insufficient training and knowledge about DevOps practices can lead to implementation challenges. Teams must understand the principles and tools involved.

4. **Tool-Centric Approach:** Focusing solely on tools without addressing cultural and process changes can lead to disappointment. Tools are essential, but they are not a silver bullet.

5. **Overemphasis on Automation:** While automation is a core aspect of DevOps, excessive automation can lead to complex and fragile systems. Not everything should be automated.

6. **Lack of Collaboration:** DevOps emphasizes collaboration between teams, but silos and lack of communication can persist, undermining the intended benefits.

7. **Ignoring Security:** DevOps should incorporate security (DevSecOps), but organizations sometimes neglect security until it becomes a problem.

8. **Scaling Too Quickly:** Rapidly scaling DevOps practices without refining processes and addressing issues can lead to chaos and instability.

Lessons from DevOps Failures

1. **Start with Clear Objectives:** Define clear and measurable objectives for your DevOps initiatives. Understand what problems you're trying to solve and how DevOps can address them.

2. **Cultural Transformation:** DevOps is not just about tools; it's a cultural transformation. Invest in cultural change, and ensure leadership supports and drives it.

3. **Education and Training:** Provide comprehensive training and education to teams involved in DevOps. Ensure they understand the principles and practices.

4. **Balanced Automation:** Strive for a balance between automation and manual processes. Not everything needs to

be automated, and human judgment is valuable.

5. **Collaboration is Key:** Foster a collaborative environment where teams work together seamlessly. Break down silos and encourage open communication.

6. **Security from the Start:** Incorporate security into DevOps practices from the beginning (DevSecOps). Address security concerns proactively.

7. **Incremental Scaling:** Scale DevOps practices gradually. Identify bottlenecks and challenges, and address them before expanding to other areas.

8. **Continuous Improvement:** DevOps is an ongoing journey. Continuously monitor, measure, and refine your processes and practices.

Case Studies: Learning from Failures

Several organizations have shared their DevOps failure stories and the lessons they've learned:

- **Knight Capital Group:** In 2012, a software deployment error cost the company $440 million in just 45 minutes. The incident highlighted the importance of rigorous testing and risk assessment before deploying changes.

- **Etsy:** The e-commerce platform Etsy experienced issues with their automated deployment process, leading to downtime and frustration for users. They learned that automation should be complemented with careful monitoring and manual intervention when necessary.

- **Amazon Web Services (AWS):** AWS faced a major outage in 2017 due to a typo during a routine debugging exercise. The incident underscored the significance of thorough testing and safeguards in automated processes.

In conclusion, DevOps failures can be valuable learning experiences. By understanding the common causes and applying the lessons learned from these failures, organizations can increase their chances of successful DevOps implementations and realize the benefits of faster, more reliable software delivery.

Chapter 17: Collaboration and Communication in DevOps Teams

Section 17.1: Effective Communication Strategies

Effective communication is at the heart of successful DevOps practices. DevOps encourages collaboration and requires cross-functional teams to work together seamlessly. In this section, we'll explore strategies for fostering effective communication within DevOps teams.

Importance of Communication in DevOps

DevOps breaks down traditional silos between development, operations, and other teams involved in the software delivery process. Effective communication is essential for several reasons:

1. **Alignment of Goals:** Teams must share a common understanding of project goals and priorities to work towards the same objectives.
2. **Quick Issue Resolution:** Rapid identification and resolution of issues are crucial for maintaining continuous delivery pipelines.
3. **Feedback Loops:** Timely feedback helps teams make improvements and catch potential problems early in the development cycle.
4. **Cross-Functional Collaboration:** Different teams with varied expertise must collaborate seamlessly to achieve DevOps success.

Strategies for Effective Communication

1. **Open and Transparent Communication:** Encourage open and transparent communication channels within teams and across departments. Transparency builds trust and ensures everyone is on the same page.

2. **Foster a Collaborative Culture:** Create a culture of collaboration where team members feel comfortable sharing ideas and feedback. Team building activities can help strengthen collaboration.

3. **Cross-Functional Teams:** DevOps teams should consist of members from various functions (e.g., development, operations, testing). This diversity promotes cross-functional knowledge sharing.

4. **Regular Stand-up Meetings:** Conduct regular stand-up meetings (e.g., daily or weekly) to discuss progress, challenges, and plans. These meetings keep everyone informed and aligned.

5. **Use Collaboration Tools:** Leverage collaboration tools like chat platforms (e.g., Slack), project management software (e.g., Jira), and version control systems (e.g., Git) to facilitate communication and document discussions.

6. **Clear Documentation:** Maintain clear and up-to-date documentation for processes, procedures, and project-related information. Documentation provides a reference point and ensures consistency.

7. **Feedback Mechanisms:** Establish feedback mechanisms where team members can provide input and raise concerns. Feedback loops are essential for continuous improvement.

8. **Effective Meetings:** When conducting meetings, ensure they have a clear agenda, goals, and a designated facilitator. Keep meetings concise and action-oriented.

9. **Empathy and Active Listening:** Encourage empathy and active listening within teams. Understanding each other's perspectives fosters better communication.

10. **Conflict Resolution:** Develop strategies for resolving conflicts constructively. Conflicts can arise when there are different opinions or priorities.

Case Studies: Successful Communication in DevOps

Several organizations have excelled in communication within their DevOps practices:

- **Netflix:** Netflix's engineering culture emphasizes freedom and responsibility. They prioritize open and honest communication, and their "Simplicity, Confidence, and Resilience" (ScaR) model encourages teams to identify and address issues quickly.

- **Amazon:** Amazon's "Two-Pizza Team" philosophy promotes small, cross-functional teams that communicate directly with each other. This structure enhances collaboration and accelerates decision-making.

- **Google:** Google's Site Reliability Engineering (SRE) teams emphasize effective communication between developers and operations teams. They use well-defined Service Level Objectives (SLOs) to set expectations and communicate reliability goals.

In summary, effective communication is a cornerstone of DevOps success. Organizations that prioritize clear, open, and collaborative communication among their teams are better positioned to reap the benefits of DevOps, including faster software delivery and improved reliability.

Section 17.2: Cross-functional Collaboration Best Practices

In DevOps, cross-functional collaboration is essential to break down organizational silos and achieve faster and more reliable software delivery. This section explores best practices for fostering effective cross-functional collaboration within DevOps teams.

Understanding Cross-Functional Collaboration

Cross-functional collaboration involves individuals from various functional areas working together to achieve a common goal. In DevOps, this typically includes developers, operations engineers, testers, security experts, and other relevant roles. The goal is to ensure that different perspectives and expertise contribute to the success of the project.

Best Practices for Cross-Functional Collaboration

1. **Shared Objectives:** Ensure that all team members share a common understanding of project objectives and key performance indicators (KPIs). This alignment helps everyone work toward the same goals.
2. **Cross-Functional Teams:** Form cross-functional teams that include members from different departments. These teams should have a clear mission and defined responsibilities.
3. **Clear Roles and Responsibilities:** Define roles and responsibilities within cross-functional teams. Everyone should know their role and how it contributes to the team's success.
4. **Effective Communication:** Promote open and transparent communication channels between team

members. Use collaboration tools and regular meetings to keep everyone informed.

5. **Empowerment:** Empower team members to make decisions within their areas of expertise. Encourage autonomy and trust among team members.

6. **Collaborative Problem-Solving:** When issues or challenges arise, encourage collaborative problem-solving. Cross-functional teams should work together to find solutions.

7. **Shared Metrics:** Define and track metrics that are relevant to all team members. Metrics can include deployment frequency, lead time, and quality indicators.

8. **Feedback Loops:** Establish feedback mechanisms within cross-functional teams. Regularly seek input from team members and iterate on processes.

9. **Cross-Training:** Promote cross-training to broaden team members' skill sets. This enables individuals to understand and appreciate the challenges and priorities of other team members.

10. **Conflict Resolution:** Develop strategies for resolving conflicts constructively. Conflicts may arise due to differing opinions or priorities, and it's important to address them openly.

Benefits of Cross-Functional Collaboration

Effective cross-functional collaboration offers several benefits:

- **Faster Delivery:** Cross-functional teams can make decisions and take action more quickly, reducing bottlenecks in the software delivery pipeline.

- **Quality Improvement:** Collaboration ensures that different perspectives contribute to improved software quality and security.

- **Reduced Silos:** Collaboration breaks down organizational silos, fostering a culture of shared responsibility.

- **Enhanced Innovation:** A diverse team with varied expertise is more likely to generate innovative solutions to problems.

- **Improved Problem-Solving:** Cross-functional collaboration enables more effective problem-solving, as different viewpoints are considered.

Case Studies: Successful Cross-Functional Collaboration

Many organizations have successfully implemented cross-functional collaboration within their DevOps practices:

- **Etsy:** Etsy's "Code as Craft" blog emphasizes the importance of cross-functional teams that include engineers, designers, and product managers. This approach has contributed to their success in continuous deployment.

- **Target:** Target's DevOps transformation involved creating cross-functional teams that included developers, operations, and quality assurance experts. This approach helped them achieve faster releases and better quality.

- **Adobe:** Adobe's DevOps journey involved breaking down silos between development and operations teams. They used cross-functional teams to streamline their release process and improve collaboration.

In conclusion, cross-functional collaboration is a fundamental aspect of DevOps. When teams from different functional areas work together effectively, they can achieve faster, more reliable software delivery and drive continuous improvement in the software development lifecycle.

Section 17.3: Role of Project Management in DevOps

In the DevOps culture, project management plays a critical role in ensuring that software development and delivery are efficient, well-coordinated, and aligned with business objectives. This section explores the role of project management in DevOps and how it contributes to the success of DevOps initiatives.

Project Management in Traditional vs. DevOps Environments

Before diving into the specifics of project management in DevOps, it's essential to understand how it differs from traditional project management approaches.

Traditional Project Management:

- Emphasizes strict planning and documentation.

- Often follows a sequential or "waterfall" approach.

- Focuses on meeting predefined milestones and deadlines.

- Limited flexibility for adapting to changes during the project.

DevOps Project Management:

- Embraces agility and flexibility.

- Encourages continuous collaboration and communication.

- Adopts an iterative and incremental approach.

- Prioritizes delivering value to users over adhering to fixed schedules.

Key Roles and Responsibilities

In a DevOps environment, project management encompasses several roles and responsibilities:

1. **Product Owner:** The product owner represents the business and user needs. They define the product backlog, prioritize features, and ensure that development efforts align with business goals.
2. **Scrum Master:** In Agile methodologies like Scrum, the Scrum Master is responsible for facilitating the development team's work, removing impediments, and ensuring adherence to Agile practices.
3. **DevOps Engineer:** A DevOps engineer may act as a project manager, focusing on automating workflows, managing infrastructure, and ensuring that deployment

pipelines run smoothly.

4. **Continuous Delivery Lead:** This role focuses on optimizing the CI/CD pipeline, monitoring release processes, and coordinating the deployment of software to production.

5. **Release Manager:** The release manager oversees the planning and execution of releases, coordinating activities across development, testing, and operations teams.

Agile Project Management in DevOps

DevOps and Agile methodologies often go hand in hand, and Agile project management practices are well-suited for DevOps environments. Some key Agile principles relevant to DevOps include:

- **Iterative Development:** DevOps encourages breaking down work into small, manageable iterations, allowing teams to continuously deliver and gather feedback.

- **Cross-Functional Teams:** Agile promotes cross-functional teams that can collectively plan, develop, test, and deploy software, aligning with DevOps principles of collaboration.

- **Customer Feedback:** Agile prioritizes customer feedback and encourages teams to adapt based on real-world user experiences, aligning with DevOps' focus on delivering value to users.

Tools and Practices

To support project management in DevOps, various tools and practices are employed:

- **Agile Frameworks:** Agile methodologies like Scrum, Kanban, or Lean provide structured approaches for managing work in DevOps teams.

- **Version Control:** Version control systems such as Git help track code changes, collaborate among team members, and maintain codebase integrity.

- **Issue Tracking:** Tools like Jira or Trello assist in managing and prioritizing work items, bugs, and new features.

- **CI/CD Pipelines:** Automation tools like Jenkins or Travis CI enable the automated building, testing, and deployment of software.

- **Collaboration Platforms:** Communication tools like Slack or Microsoft Teams facilitate real-time communication and collaboration among team members.

Benefits of Effective Project Management in DevOps

Effective project management in DevOps offers several advantages:

- **Enhanced Collaboration:** Well-coordinated teams collaborate more effectively, leading to faster delivery and higher-quality software.

- **Adaptability:** DevOps project management embraces change and allows teams to adapt to evolving requirements and priorities.

- **Efficiency:** Automation and streamlined workflows improve efficiency, reducing manual and error-prone tasks.

- **Transparency:** Clear communication and visibility into project progress enable stakeholders to make informed decisions.

- **Customer Satisfaction:** Delivering features and updates more frequently leads to improved customer satisfaction.

In conclusion, project management plays a pivotal role in the success of DevOps initiatives. By adopting Agile principles, leveraging appropriate tools, and fostering collaboration, project managers contribute to the continuous improvement and delivery of value in DevOps environments.

Section 17.4: Building High-Performing DevOps Teams

Building high-performing DevOps teams is crucial for the success of DevOps initiatives. In this section, we will explore strategies and practices to create teams that excel in delivering value, fostering collaboration, and driving continuous improvement.

Characteristics of High-Performing DevOps Teams

High-performing DevOps teams exhibit several key characteristics that set them apart:

1. **Collaboration:** Team members work closely together, breaking down silos between development, operations, and other functions. Effective communication and shared goals

are fundamental.

2. **Automation Proficiency:** High-performing teams automate repetitive tasks, from code builds and testing to deployment and infrastructure provisioning. Automation accelerates delivery and reduces errors.

3. **Continuous Learning:** DevOps is an ever-evolving field, and high-performing teams embrace a culture of continuous learning. They stay up-to-date with new technologies and industry best practices.

4. **Empowerment:** Team members are empowered to make decisions and take ownership of their work. This autonomy fosters innovation and a sense of responsibility.

5. **Feedback-Driven:** High-performing teams actively seek feedback from users and stakeholders. They use feedback to improve processes and products iteratively.

6. **Metrics-Driven:** Metrics and key performance indicators (KPIs) are used to measure and monitor the success of DevOps processes. Teams regularly analyze these metrics to identify areas for improvement.

Strategies for Building High-Performing DevOps Teams

1. Cross-Functional Teams: Form teams with a mix of skills, including developers, operations, quality assurance, and security experts. Cross-functional teams can independently plan, build, test, and deploy software.

2. Training and Skill Development: Invest in training and skill development programs to ensure that team members have the necessary expertise in DevOps tools and practices.

3. Mentoring and Knowledge Sharing: Encourage senior team members to mentor less experienced ones. Foster a culture of knowledge sharing through pair programming, tech talks, and documentation.

4. Empowerment and Ownership: Give team members the autonomy to make decisions related to their work. When individuals feel ownership, they are more invested in the team's success.

5. Clear Goals and Priorities: Define clear goals and priorities for the team. Ensure that everyone understands the overall mission and how their work contributes to it.

6. Foster a Culture of Experimentation: Encourage experimentation and risk-taking. Provide a safe environment where failures are seen as opportunities for learning and improvement.

7. Automate Repetitive Tasks: Identify tasks that can be

*automated and implement automation tools and scripts. This frees
up time for more strategic work.*

*8. Feedback Loops: Establish feedback loops with stakeholders,
end-users, and between team members. Use feedback to refine
processes and make data-driven decisions.*

*9. Metrics for Improvement: Define and track key metrics related
to DevOps processes, such as deployment frequency, lead time, and
change failure rate. Regularly review these metrics and set
improvement goals.*

*10. Celebrate Achievements: Recognize and celebrate team
achievements and milestones. Acknowledging hard work and
successes boosts team morale.*

Challenges and Continuous Improvement

Building and maintaining high-performing DevOps teams is an
ongoing journey. Challenges may arise, such as team turnover,
tooling issues, or changing business priorities. However, with a
commitment to continuous improvement and a focus on the core
principles of DevOps, teams can adapt and thrive in dynamic
environments.

In conclusion, high-performing DevOps teams are characterized by
collaboration, automation, continuous learning, and a focus on
delivering value. Building such teams requires a combination of
strategic planning, skill development, and a culture that values
experimentation and feedback. These teams are well-equipped to
drive innovation and meet the demands of modern software
development.

Section 17.5: Case Studies: Successful Team Dynamics

In this section, we will delve into real-world case studies that highlight successful team dynamics within DevOps environments. These examples will showcase how different organizations have implemented DevOps principles and practices to achieve remarkable results.

Case Study 1: Company X - Transforming Silos into Collaboration

Background: Company X, a large enterprise, faced challenges with siloed development and operations teams, leading to slow releases, frequent errors, and poor communication.

DevOps Transformation: Company X initiated a DevOps transformation by creating cross-functional teams consisting of developers, operations engineers, and quality assurance experts. They adopted automation tools for testing, deployment, and infrastructure provisioning.

Results: By breaking down silos and promoting collaboration, Company X achieved a 50% reduction in deployment times and a 40% decrease in post-release incidents. The improved communication and shared responsibility among teams resulted in higher-quality software and faster delivery.

Case Study 2: Startup Y - DevOps from Day One

Background: Startup Y, a technology startup, recognized the importance of DevOps from its inception. They aimed to build a culture of automation, agility, and rapid delivery.

DevOps Implementation: Startup Y established a cloud-native infrastructure using Infrastructure as Code (IaC) and containerization. They implemented a CI/CD pipeline for automated testing and deployment.

Results: With DevOps practices ingrained in their culture, Startup Y achieved rapid feature delivery and scalability. They reduced infrastructure costs by 30% through efficient resource management. This approach allowed them to quickly respond to market demands and gain a competitive edge.

Case Study 3: Organization Z - Continuous Improvement and Learning

Background: Organization Z, a medium-sized company, had an existing DevOps practice but sought to enhance it further.

DevOps Enhancement: Organization Z emphasized continuous learning and improvement. They introduced regular retrospectives to identify areas of improvement, encouraged employees to attend training and certification programs, and allocated time for innovation projects.

Results: The focus on continuous improvement led to a 20% increase in deployment frequency. Teams identified bottlenecks and inefficiencies, resulting in streamlined processes and faster releases. Employee satisfaction and retention improved due to the emphasis on skill development and personal growth.

Case Study 4: E-commerce Giant W - Managing Peak Loads

Background: E-commerce Giant W faced challenges during peak shopping seasons when their website experienced high traffic loads.

DevOps Solutions: To handle peak loads, E-commerce Giant W implemented auto-scaling capabilities in their cloud infrastructure. They utilized container orchestration for scalability and employed real-time monitoring to detect issues proactively.

Results: During peak seasons, the website's performance remained consistent, and downtime was virtually eliminated. E-commerce Giant W reported a 25% increase in revenue during peak periods, and customer satisfaction improved significantly.

Case Study 5: Healthcare Provider V - DevOps for Critical Applications

Background: Healthcare Provider V needed to ensure the reliability and security of critical healthcare applications while keeping pace with technological advancements.

DevOps Approach: They adopted a "DevSecOps" approach, integrating security into the DevOps lifecycle. Automated security testing was implemented as part of the CI/CD pipeline. Regular compliance audits were conducted to meet industry standards.

Results: Healthcare Provider V achieved enhanced security and compliance, reducing the risk of data breaches. Their applications remained available and reliable, even during security updates. The organization gained trust from patients and partners and remained at the forefront of healthcare technology.

These case studies demonstrate the diverse ways in which DevOps principles and practices can be tailored to suit the unique needs of different organizations. Whether it's breaking down silos, embracing DevOps from the start, emphasizing continuous improvement, managing peak loads, or prioritizing security, successful team dynamics play a pivotal role in achieving remarkable outcomes.

Organizations that invest in DevOps and foster a culture of collaboration and innovation are well-positioned for success in today's competitive landscape.

Chapter 18: Continuous Learning and Skill Development

Section 18.1: Keeping Up with Evolving DevOps Practices

In the ever-evolving landscape of DevOps, staying current with the latest practices, tools, and technologies is crucial for professionals and organizations to remain competitive and efficient. This section explores the importance of continuous learning and provides strategies to keep up with the dynamic field of DevOps.

The Rapid Evolution of DevOps

DevOps is characterized by its rapid evolution, driven by changes in technology, market demands, and best practices. What was considered cutting-edge in DevOps a few years ago may now be outdated. As a result, keeping up with the latest developments is essential.

Strategies for Staying Informed

1. Continuous Reading and Research:

- DevOps professionals should dedicate time to read blogs, articles, and books related to DevOps practices.

- Engaging with online DevOps communities and forums is an excellent way to share knowledge and gain insights.

2. Attend Conferences and Meetups:

- DevOps conferences and local meetups provide opportunities to network with peers and learn from industry experts.

- These events often feature presentations, workshops, and hands-on experiences with the latest DevOps tools.

3. Online Courses and Certifications:

- Enrolling in online courses and obtaining relevant certifications can provide structured learning paths.

- Platforms like Coursera, edX, and Udemy offer courses on various DevOps topics.

4. Participate in Webinars and Podcasts:

- Webinars and podcasts offer a convenient way to learn from experts and stay updated on industry trends.

- Many DevOps thought leaders host webinars and podcasts regularly.

5. Hands-On Practice:

- Practical experience is invaluable in DevOps. Professionals should experiment with new tools and techniques in a sandbox environment.

- Contributions to open-source projects can provide hands-on learning opportunities.

Creating a Learning Culture

Organizations should encourage a culture of continuous learning to keep their DevOps teams up to date. This includes:

- Allocating time for training and skill development in employees' schedules.

- Supporting attendance at conferences, webinars, and courses.

- Recognizing and rewarding employees for gaining new skills and certifications.

- Encouraging knowledge sharing within the team through regular meetings or brown bag sessions.

Monitoring Emerging Trends

DevOps practitioners should monitor emerging trends and technologies, such as:

- **GitOps:** The use of Git as a single source of truth for infrastructure and application deployment.

- **Serverless Computing:** Leveraging serverless platforms for event-driven application execution.

- **AIOps:** The integration of artificial intelligence and machine learning into IT operations.

- **Immutable Infrastructure:** Treating infrastructure as code to enable rapid, consistent deployments.

Conclusion

In the dynamic world of DevOps, continuous learning is not an option; it's a necessity. By staying informed, attending events, obtaining certifications, and fostering a culture of learning, both individuals and organizations can adapt to the evolving DevOps landscape and drive innovation in software development and operations.

Section 18.2: Training and Certification in DevOps

Training and certification play a significant role in the professional development of individuals and teams in the DevOps field. In this section, we will explore the importance of DevOps training and certification, the various certification programs available, and how they can benefit both individuals and organizations.

The Significance of DevOps Training and Certification

1. Standardization of Knowledge:

- DevOps certifications provide a standardized way to evaluate and validate the knowledge and skills of professionals.

- They help ensure that practitioners have a common understanding of DevOps principles and practices.

2. Career Advancement:

- Having DevOps certifications can enhance an individual's career prospects.

- Employers often look for certified professionals as they demonstrate a commitment to continuous learning and skill development.

3. Competitive Edge:

- In a competitive job market, certifications can set candidates apart from others.

- They showcase expertise and a deeper understanding of DevOps concepts.

4. Knowledge Expansion:

- DevOps training programs cover a wide range of topics, from tools and automation to culture and collaboration.

- Professionals can gain a holistic view of DevOps through these programs.

Popular DevOps Certifications

1. AWS Certified DevOps Engineer:

- Offered by Amazon Web Services, this certification focuses on DevOps practices in the AWS ecosystem.

- It covers automation, security, and best practices for deploying and managing applications on AWS.

2. Certified Kubernetes Administrator (CKA):

- This certification, provided by the Cloud Native Computing Foundation (CNCF), validates skills in Kubernetes administration.

- Kubernetes is a critical component in container orchestration, a key DevOps area.

3. Certified Jenkins Engineer (CJE):

- Jenkins is a widely-used automation server in DevOps. This certification tests expertise in Jenkins usage and administration.

4. Certified Docker Associate (CDA):

- Docker is a fundamental technology in containerization and DevOps. This certification assesses knowledge of Docker fundamentals.

5. DevOps Institute Certifications:

- DevOps Institute offers various certifications, including DevOps Foundation, DevSecOps Engineering, and more.

- These certifications cover a broad spectrum of DevOps topics and practices.

How Organizations Benefit

1. Skilled Workforce:

- Certified employees are equipped with up-to-date knowledge and skills, contributing to the organization's success.

2. Efficient Processes:

- DevOps certification helps teams implement best practices, streamline processes, and reduce operational costs.

3. Competitive Advantage:

- Organizations with certified DevOps professionals gain a competitive advantage in delivering software faster and with higher quality.

4. Improved Collaboration:

- Certified team members are more likely to embrace DevOps culture and collaborate effectively.

Preparing for DevOps Certification

1. Training Courses:

- Many certification providers offer official training courses that cover the exam objectives.

- These courses may be instructor-led or available online.

2. Practice Exams:

- Practice exams simulate the certification test environment and help candidates assess their readiness.

3. Self-Study:

- DevOps professionals can also prepare for certifications through self-study using books, documentation, and online resources.

Conclusion

DevOps training and certification are essential components of professional growth and organizational success. They validate expertise, enhance career prospects, and enable individuals and teams to stay current with DevOps practices and technologies. As DevOps continues to evolve, staying certified demonstrates a commitment to excellence and continuous improvement in the field.

Section 18.3: Learning Resources and Communities

In the world of DevOps, continuous learning is not just a practice but a necessity. Staying updated with the latest trends, tools, and best practices is crucial for professionals and teams. This section explores various learning resources and communities that can aid in ongoing DevOps education and skill enhancement.

DevOps Learning Resources

1. Online Courses and MOOCs:

- Platforms like Coursera, edX, Udemy, and Pluralsight offer a plethora of DevOps-related courses.

- These courses cover a wide range of topics, from DevOps culture to specific tools like Docker and Kubernetes.

2. DevOps Books:

- There are numerous books available on DevOps, catering to different levels of expertise.

- Some popular titles include "The Phoenix Project" by Gene Kim, "Continuous Delivery" by Jez Humble and David Farley, and "Site Reliability Engineering" by Niall Richard Murphy, Betsy Beyer, and others.

3. Documentation and Blogs:

- Official documentation of DevOps tools and platforms is a valuable resource.

- Many experts and practitioners maintain blogs sharing their experiences and insights, providing practical knowledge.

4. YouTube Channels and Webinars:

- DevOps-related YouTube channels and webinars offer video tutorials, demos, and discussions.

- They are a visual way to learn and gain insights from experts in the field.

5. Podcasts:

- DevOps podcasts like "DevOps Radio," "Arrested DevOps," and "The Ship Show" feature interviews, discussions, and real-world experiences.

6. DevOps Forums and Q&A Websites:

- Communities like Stack Overflow, Reddit's r/devops, and DevOps Stack Exchange are excellent for asking questions and sharing knowledge.

DevOps Communities

1. Meetups and User Groups:

- DevOps meetups and user groups are held in many cities globally.

- These events provide networking opportunities and a chance to learn from local experts.

2. Online Forums:

- DevOps forums like Dev.to and DevOpsChat.io are virtual spaces where professionals can engage in discussions, seek advice, and share insights.

3. LinkedIn Groups:

- Numerous LinkedIn groups are dedicated to DevOps discussions and networking.

- Joining these groups allows professionals to connect with peers and industry leaders.

4. Social Media:

- Twitter and other social media platforms have active DevOps communities.

- Following DevOps practitioners and thought leaders can provide a steady stream of industry updates.

Continuous Learning Strategies

1. Set Learning Goals:

- Define what you want to learn and achieve in your DevOps journey.

- Having clear goals will help you focus your learning efforts.

2. Stay Curious:

- Embrace curiosity and a growth mindset.

- Be open to exploring new tools, practices, and technologies.

3. Practice, Experiment, and Build:

- Learning by doing is often the most effective method.

- Create personal projects to apply your DevOps skills.

4. Collaborate and Share:

- Engage with the DevOps community, both online and offline.

- Sharing knowledge and experiences benefits both you and the community.

5. Stay Informed:

- Subscribe to newsletters, blogs, and podcasts to stay updated.

- DevOps is a rapidly evolving field, and staying informed is crucial.

6. Certifications and Courses:

- Consider enrolling in DevOps certification programs and courses to gain structured knowledge.

Conclusion

Continuous learning is at the core of DevOps culture. The DevOps field is dynamic, and professionals need to adapt to new tools and practices regularly. By leveraging a wide range of learning resources and participating in DevOps communities, individuals and teams can stay at the forefront of the industry and contribute to their organizations' success. Remember that in DevOps, the journey of learning is as important as the destination, and the collaborative spirit of the community is a powerful driving force.

Section 18.4: Encouraging a Learning Culture in DevOps Teams

A learning culture is a fundamental aspect of any successful DevOps team. It promotes continuous improvement, innovation, and the ability to adapt to new challenges. In this section, we'll explore the importance of fostering a learning culture within DevOps teams and how to encourage it effectively.

The Value of a Learning Culture

1. **Adaptability:** In a rapidly evolving field like DevOps, the ability to learn and adapt quickly is critical. A learning culture equips teams to embrace change and stay ahead of emerging trends and technologies.
2. **Increased Efficiency:** Continuous learning leads to process optimization and the elimination of bottlenecks. This, in turn, improves the efficiency of DevOps pipelines and delivery.
3. **Innovation:** Learning cultures encourage experimentation and innovation. Team members are more likely to propose and implement novel solutions to challenges.

4. **Employee Engagement:** DevOps professionals are more engaged when they have opportunities for skill development and growth. This can lead to higher job satisfaction and retention.

5. **Problem Solving:** A learning culture fosters problem-solving skills. Team members are better equipped to identify issues, analyze root causes, and find effective solutions.

Strategies for Encouraging a Learning Culture

1. **Lead by Example:** Team leaders and managers should set the tone by actively engaging in learning activities and sharing their knowledge.

2. **Provide Resources:** Ensure that team members have access to the necessary learning resources, such as courses, books, and subscriptions to relevant platforms.

3. **Allocate Time:** Dedicate time for learning during work hours. This can include weekly "learning hours" or days set aside for skill development.

4. **Encourage Knowledge Sharing:** Create a culture of knowledge sharing where team members are encouraged to share what they've learned with their colleagues.

5. **Recognize and Reward Learning:** Acknowledge and reward team members who invest in their learning and apply new skills to benefit the team.

6. **Regular Feedback:** Provide constructive feedback on team members' learning efforts and help them set achievable learning goals.

7. **Cross-Training:** Encourage cross-training within the team, where members share expertise in different areas of DevOps.

8. **Hackathons and Challenges:** Organize hackathons or

challenges that require teams to learn and implement new technologies or practices.

9. **Learning Communities:** Join and support external learning communities, such as DevOps meetups or online forums, and encourage team members to participate.

10. **Continuous Improvement:** Continuously assess the effectiveness of your learning initiatives and adjust them based on feedback and results.

Challenges and Solutions

Implementing a learning culture in DevOps teams may face some challenges:

- **Time Constraints:** DevOps teams are often busy with day-to-day tasks. To overcome this, allocate dedicated learning time and balance it with operational responsibilities.

- **Resistance to Change:** Some team members may resist adopting a learning culture. Address this by showcasing the benefits of learning and providing support.

- **Resource Limitations:** Ensure that the team has access to the necessary learning resources, even if it requires budget allocation.

- **Measuring Impact:** It can be challenging to measure the direct impact of a learning culture on productivity. Focus on key performance indicators (KPIs) related to efficiency, innovation, and problem-solving.

- **Sustainability:** A learning culture should be sustainable in the long term. Make it an integral part of the team's values and practices.

In conclusion, a learning culture is a key driver of success in DevOps teams. By embracing continuous learning and providing the necessary support and resources, organizations can empower their teams to excel in a rapidly evolving field and drive innovation in software development and delivery.

Section 18.5: Personal Development Plans for DevOps Professionals

Personal development plans (PDPs) are essential tools for fostering growth and career advancement in DevOps. In this section, we will explore the significance of personal development plans for DevOps professionals and how to create effective PDPs tailored to individual career goals.

Importance of Personal Development Plans

1. **Goal Alignment:** Personal development plans help align an individual's career aspirations with the organization's objectives. This ensures that employees' growth contributes to the company's success.
2. **Skill Enhancement:** PDPs facilitate the identification of skills gaps and the development of strategies to acquire new skills or enhance existing ones. This is particularly valuable in a field as dynamic as DevOps.
3. **Motivation:** Setting clear goals and milestones through PDPs can be motivating for employees. It provides a sense of purpose and direction in their career.
4. **Performance Improvement:** Regular self-assessment and

goal tracking enable employees to gauge their progress and make necessary adjustments to improve their performance.

5. **Retention and Engagement:** Companies that invest in the professional growth of their employees are more likely to retain top talent and keep them engaged in their roles.

Creating Effective Personal Development Plans

Here are steps to create effective personal development plans for DevOps professionals:

1. Self-Assessment

Begin by conducting a thorough self-assessment. Identify your strengths, weaknesses, interests, and career aspirations. Consider your current skills and the skills required for your desired role.

2. Set Clear Goals

Based on your self-assessment, establish clear and specific career goals. Ensure that these goals are aligned with your organization's objectives and your personal aspirations.

3. Identify Skill Gaps

Identify the skills and knowledge gaps that need to be addressed to achieve your goals. These gaps may include technical skills, soft skills, or domain-specific knowledge.

4. Plan Learning Activities

Outline a plan for acquiring or enhancing the necessary skills. This may involve enrolling in courses, attending workshops, seeking mentorship, or participating in relevant projects within your organization.

5. Establish Milestones

Break down your goals into smaller, achievable milestones. This makes it easier to track your progress and stay motivated.

6. Allocate Resources

Determine the resources required for your development, such as time, budget, and access to learning materials. Ensure that you have the necessary support from your organization.

7. Seek Feedback

Regularly seek feedback from mentors, managers, or colleagues to assess your progress and receive guidance on your development journey.

8. Adapt and Iterate

Be flexible and willing to adapt your PDP as needed. DevOps is a fast-changing field, and your goals may evolve along with industry trends.

9. Measure Success

Define key performance indicators (KPIs) to measure the success of your PDP. These may include certifications achieved, projects completed, or improvements in specific skills.

10. *Reflect and Celebrate*

Periodically reflect on your achievements and celebrate your successes, no matter how small. This can boost your motivation and morale.

Challenges and Considerations

DevOps professionals may encounter challenges in creating and implementing PDPs, including time constraints, resource limitations, and changing career goals. To address these challenges, it's essential to maintain flexibility and adaptability in your plan.

In conclusion, personal development plans are powerful tools for DevOps professionals to advance their careers, acquire new skills, and stay competitive in the industry. By following a structured approach and regularly reviewing and updating their PDPs, individuals can achieve their career goals and contribute effectively to their organizations' DevOps initiatives.

Section 19.1: DevOps in Different Industries

DevOps practices and principles have found application and success across a wide range of industries. In this section, we'll explore how various sectors, from finance to healthcare, have embraced DevOps to improve their operations, enhance product delivery, and stay competitive in the digital age.

Finance and Banking

The finance and banking industry has undergone a significant transformation with the adoption of DevOps. Traditional financial institutions have embraced automation, continuous delivery, and cloud technologies to streamline processes, reduce errors, and enhance customer experiences. DevOps practices have enabled faster and more reliable software releases for online banking, trading platforms, and mobile applications. Furthermore, security and compliance are paramount in this industry, and DevSecOps practices have become instrumental in ensuring the safety of financial transactions and data.

Healthcare

In healthcare, DevOps has revolutionized the way software is developed and deployed. Electronic health record (EHR) systems, telemedicine platforms, and medical device software require frequent updates and rigorous testing. DevOps enables healthcare organizations to deliver updates quickly, ensuring that critical systems remain secure and efficient. Moreover, it supports compliance with healthcare regulations, such as the Health Insurance Portability and Accountability Act (HIPAA), by automating auditing and reporting processes.

E-commerce and Retail

E-commerce and retail companies rely heavily on technology to provide seamless online shopping experiences. DevOps practices have allowed them to scale their infrastructure during peak shopping seasons, implement continuous integration and delivery (CI/CD) pipelines for faster updates, and leverage data analytics for personalized recommendations. These efforts have led to improved customer satisfaction and increased sales.

Entertainment and Media

The entertainment and media industry leverages DevOps to manage content delivery, streaming platforms, and content recommendation engines. DevOps practices enable real-time updates of streaming services, ensuring uninterrupted viewing experiences for users. Additionally, A/B testing and analytics help optimize content recommendations, keeping viewers engaged.

Gaming

In the gaming industry, DevOps supports the development and maintenance of online multiplayer games, game servers, and gaming platforms. DevOps teams manage game updates, server maintenance, and player data, ensuring a smooth gaming experience. Continuous monitoring and automation are crucial for identifying and resolving performance issues, maintaining player trust, and preventing downtime.

Automotive and Manufacturing

Automotive manufacturers have integrated DevOps practices into their processes, particularly in software-driven components such as infotainment systems, autonomous driving features, and vehicle management systems. DevOps ensures the rapid development and deployment of software updates to improve vehicle performance, safety, and user experience. Additionally, it enables remote diagnostics and over-the-air (OTA) updates, reducing the need for physical recalls.

Government and Public Sector

Government agencies and the public sector have adopted DevOps to modernize their IT infrastructure, enhance citizen services, and increase operational efficiency. DevOps practices help deliver government applications and services faster, reduce costs, and ensure security and compliance. Furthermore, they enable agencies to respond swiftly to changing requirements, such as disaster management and public health emergencies.

Conclusion

DevOps principles and practices have transcended industry boundaries, driving innovation, efficiency, and agility in various sectors. Organizations across finance, healthcare, e-commerce, entertainment, gaming, automotive, government, and more have realized the value of DevOps in meeting the demands of the digital age. As technology continues to evolve, DevOps will remain a crucial component of staying competitive and delivering high-quality products and services to customers and citizens alike.

Section 19.2: Regional DevOps Practices and Trends

DevOps practices have spread globally, but regional variations and trends exist based on unique technological landscapes, cultural influences, and economic factors. In this section, we'll explore some of the regional variations in DevOps adoption and practices.

North America

North America, particularly the United States, has been at the forefront of DevOps adoption. Silicon Valley, known for its tech innovation, has played a pivotal role in shaping DevOps practices. Continuous integration, containerization, and cloud adoption have been prevalent. Companies here have focused on automation to improve speed and efficiency. DevOps culture emphasizes collaboration, with a strong presence of DevOps meetups and conferences.

Europe

DevOps adoption in Europe varies by country and industry. Countries like Germany and the UK have embraced DevOps practices in manufacturing, automotive, and finance. The European Union's General Data Protection Regulation (GDPR) has driven DevSecOps practices to ensure data protection and compliance. The DevOps community is active, organizing events and sharing best practices.

Asia-Pacific

Asia-Pacific (APAC) countries have seen a surge in DevOps adoption, with India and Australia leading the way. Rapidly growing technology markets and a focus on digital transformation have accelerated DevOps adoption. However, cultural differences and language barriers can impact collaboration. APAC organizations often focus on cost-effective solutions and scaling DevOps practices across diverse teams.

Latin America

DevOps adoption in Latin America is on the rise, driven by industries like banking, e-commerce, and telecommunications. Brazil and Mexico have active DevOps communities. Limited access to resources and talent can be a challenge, but organizations are investing in training and skill development. Localization and cultural awareness are important factors in successful DevOps implementations.

Middle East and Africa

The Middle East and Africa (MEA) region are experiencing a growing interest in DevOps, particularly in the Gulf Cooperation Council (GCC) countries. Government initiatives and a push for digital transformation have spurred DevOps adoption. Organizations are investing in cloud infrastructure and automation to improve service delivery. Cybersecurity and data privacy are key concerns, leading to a focus on DevSecOps practices.

Conclusion

DevOps practices have become a global phenomenon, with each region adapting them to suit their unique needs and challenges. While common principles like automation, collaboration, and continuous delivery remain universal, the specific tools, technologies, and cultural nuances vary from one region to another. The global DevOps community continues to grow, sharing experiences and knowledge to drive innovation and excellence in software development and IT operations worldwide.

Section 19.3: Global Collaboration in DevOps Projects

DevOps practices thrive on collaboration, and in today's interconnected world, global collaboration is a defining feature. Organizations are no longer limited by geographical boundaries, and software development and IT operations have become truly global endeavors. In this section, we'll explore how global collaboration is transforming DevOps projects.

Distributed Teams

One of the most significant changes in DevOps is the rise of distributed teams. Organizations can tap into talent pools from around the world, assembling teams with diverse skill sets. Tools like video conferencing, instant messaging, and project management software facilitate seamless communication and collaboration among team members spread across different time zones.

24/7 Operations

Global collaboration enables 24/7 operations. With teams working in different time zones, development and operations activities can continue around the clock. This results in faster development cycles, quicker issue resolution, and improved service availability. It also aligns with the principle of continuous delivery, where updates can be deployed at any time without causing disruptions.

Cultural Diversity

Global collaboration brings together professionals from various cultural backgrounds. While this diversity can lead to creative problem-solving and innovative ideas, it also requires cultural sensitivity and awareness. Understanding different work styles, communication norms, and expectations is crucial for effective collaboration. DevOps teams must foster an inclusive culture that values diversity and promotes equal participation.

Tools and Infrastructure

Cloud computing and Infrastructure as Code (IaC) have been instrumental in supporting global collaboration. Cloud providers offer data centers in multiple regions, allowing organizations to deploy resources closer to their target audiences. IaC tools enable the automated provisioning and management of infrastructure, ensuring consistency across regions. Additionally, version control systems and collaboration platforms facilitate code sharing and documentation across distributed teams.

Challenges and Solutions

While global collaboration offers numerous advantages, it also presents challenges. Language barriers, differences in work cultures, and time zone misalignments can lead to misunderstandings and delays. To address these challenges, organizations should invest in cross-cultural training, establish clear communication protocols, and implement Agile and DevOps best practices that prioritize transparency and feedback.

Case Studies

Several successful companies have embraced global collaboration in their DevOps journey. For example, multinational corporations like IBM and Microsoft have distributed DevOps teams across the globe, leveraging local expertise and resources. Startups like GitHub, now a part of Microsoft, have a global user base and a distributed team that contributes to open-source projects.

In conclusion, global collaboration is reshaping the DevOps landscape. It enables organizations to access a global talent pool, operate around the clock, and leverage cultural diversity for innovation. While it presents challenges, proactive measures and the right tools can overcome them. DevOps teams that embrace global collaboration are well-positioned to thrive in an interconnected world, delivering high-quality software and services to a global audience.

Section 19.4: The Role of DevOps in Digital Transformation

Digital transformation is a strategic imperative for organizations across industries, and DevOps plays a pivotal role in this journey. In this section, we will explore how DevOps contributes to and accelerates the process of digital transformation.

Defining Digital Transformation

Digital transformation involves the integration of digital technology into all aspects of an organization, fundamentally changing how it operates and delivers value to customers. It encompasses a wide range of initiatives, from automating manual processes to creating innovative digital products and services. The ultimate goal is to become more agile, customer-centric, and competitive in the digital age.

The Connection Between DevOps and Digital Transformation

DevOps aligns perfectly with the goals of digital transformation. Here's how DevOps contributes to this transformation:

1. Speed and Agility

DevOps practices emphasize automation, continuous integration, and continuous delivery (CI/CD), enabling organizations to develop, test, and deploy software faster. This agility is crucial in responding to changing market conditions, customer demands, and competitive pressures. Faster releases mean quicker time-to-market for digital products and services.

2. Collaboration and Communication

Digital transformation often involves breaking down silos within an organization and fostering collaboration among different teams. DevOps promotes a culture of collaboration and transparent communication between development, operations, and other stakeholders. This collaboration extends beyond teams to include partners and customers, facilitating the co-creation of digital solutions.

3. Quality and Reliability

Digital transformation is not just about speed; it's also about delivering high-quality, reliable digital experiences. DevOps practices, such as automated testing, monitoring, and feedback loops, ensure that software meets performance, security, and reliability standards. This is critical in building and maintaining trust with digital consumers.

4. Scalability and Efficiency

Scalability is a key component of digital transformation, as organizations need to handle growing workloads and user demands. Cloud computing and containerization, which are often part of DevOps toolchains, provide the scalability and efficiency required for digital services. Resources can be provisioned and scaled dynamically to meet demand.

5. Data-Driven Decision-Making

Digital transformation relies on data-driven insights to make informed decisions. DevOps practices emphasize metrics and analytics, enabling organizations to gather data on software performance, user behavior, and other key indicators. This data can inform strategic decisions and drive continuous improvement.

Case Studies

Many organizations have successfully leveraged DevOps as a catalyst for their digital transformation efforts. Companies like Amazon,

Netflix, and Google have set industry standards by adopting DevOps practices to deliver innovative digital services at scale. These case studies serve as inspirations for other organizations seeking to embark on their digital transformation journeys.

Challenges

While DevOps contributes significantly to digital transformation, it's not without challenges. Cultural resistance, legacy systems, and the need for organizational change management can pose hurdles. However, addressing these challenges is essential for reaping the benefits of DevOps in a digital transformation context.

In conclusion, DevOps and digital transformation are tightly intertwined. DevOps practices empower organizations to accelerate their digital initiatives, become more agile, and deliver high-quality digital products and services. Embracing DevOps principles is not just a technical choice but a strategic one for organizations looking to thrive in the digital age.

Section 19.5: Future Prospects of DevOps Worldwide

As DevOps continues to evolve, it is essential to look ahead and consider its future prospects on a global scale. In this section, we will explore the potential trends and developments that may shape the future of DevOps worldwide.

1. Expansion Across Industries

DevOps has already made significant inroads in the IT and software development sectors. In the future, we can expect its expansion across various industries, including finance, healthcare, manufacturing, and more. The principles of automation, collaboration, and continuous improvement are applicable in diverse domains.

2. DevOps in Small and Medium Enterprises (SMEs)

While large enterprises have been early adopters of DevOps, SMEs are increasingly recognizing its benefits. As tooling becomes more accessible and DevOps practices mature, SMEs will embrace DevOps to improve their development processes, enhance competitiveness, and deliver high-quality products and services.

3. The Role of Artificial Intelligence (AI)

AI integration with DevOps will continue to grow. Machine learning algorithms will be used for predictive analytics, anomaly detection, and automation of routine tasks. AI-driven insights will help teams make data-driven decisions and further optimize DevOps pipelines.

4. Serverless and Edge Computing

Serverless and edge computing will gain prominence in DevOps practices. These technologies enable organizations to deploy functions and services closer to end-users, reducing latency and improving user experiences. DevOps teams will need to adapt their workflows to manage serverless deployments efficiently.

5. Enhanced Security Integration

DevSecOps, the integration of security into DevOps practices, will become even more critical. Security automation, continuous vulnerability assessments, and proactive threat detection will be integral parts of DevOps pipelines. With the increasing emphasis on cybersecurity, DevSecOps will play a pivotal role in safeguarding digital assets.

6. Cross-Platform and Multi-Cloud Deployments

As organizations adopt multi-cloud and hybrid cloud strategies, DevOps practices will need to accommodate cross-platform deployments. DevOps engineers will focus on ensuring seamless integration between various cloud providers and on-premises infrastructure.

7. Regulatory Compliance and Governance

In an era of stringent data privacy regulations, DevOps will need to address compliance and governance challenges more comprehensively. DevOps tooling will incorporate features for auditing, tracking changes, and ensuring adherence to regulatory requirements.

8. Continuous Learning and Certification

The DevOps landscape evolves rapidly, and professionals will need to stay up-to-date with the latest tools and practices. Continuous learning and professional certification programs will gain importance as organizations seek skilled DevOps practitioners.

9. Global Collaboration

DevOps teams will collaborate globally, leveraging distributed talent pools. Tools for remote work, virtual collaboration, and cultural diversity will be essential for fostering effective cross-border teamwork.

10. Sustainability and Green DevOps

Environmental concerns will influence DevOps practices. Green DevOps initiatives will focus on optimizing resource utilization, reducing carbon footprints, and adopting eco-friendly technology solutions.

In conclusion, the future of DevOps is promising and dynamic. As organizations worldwide recognize the value of DevOps in accelerating software delivery, enhancing quality, and achieving business objectives, its adoption will continue to grow. The integration of emerging technologies, increased focus on security and compliance, and global collaboration will be key drivers of DevOps evolution on a global scale. Staying attuned to these trends will be crucial for organizations and professionals to thrive in the ever-evolving DevOps landscape.

Chapter 20: Preparing for the Future of DevOps

Section 20.1: Emerging Technologies and Trends in DevOps

As we step into the future of DevOps, it is essential to be aware of the emerging technologies and trends that are poised to shape the landscape. In this section, we will explore some of the key developments that DevOps professionals and organizations should prepare for.

1. GitOps

GitOps is an approach that extends the principles of Git version control to infrastructure and application delivery. It emphasizes the use of declarative configuration files stored in Git repositories to manage infrastructure and application deployments. This approach enhances visibility, traceability, and automation, making it easier to maintain and scale infrastructure.

apiVersion: apps/v1

kind: Deployment

metadata:

name: my-app

spec:

replicas: 3

template:

```
metadata:

labels:

app: my-app

spec:

containers:

- name: my-app-container

image: my-app:v1.0.0
```

2. Progressive Delivery

Progressive delivery builds upon the concepts of continuous delivery and deployment by introducing gradual and controlled releases. It allows organizations to roll out new features and updates to a subset of users, gather feedback, and progressively expand the release to a broader audience. Techniques like feature flags and canary deployments are central to progressive delivery.

```
if (featureFlags.isEnabled('new-feature')) {

// Render and enable the new feature for a subset of users

renderNewFeature();

} else {

// Display the existing functionality for other users

renderOldFeature();

}
```

3. Infrastructure as Code (IaC) Evolution

IaC will continue to evolve with a focus on simplification and automation. Frameworks like AWS Cloud Development Kit (CDK) and Pulumi enable developers to define infrastructure using familiar programming languages, further blurring the lines between application and infrastructure code.

```
import * as aws from 'aws-cdk-lib/aws';

const bucket = new aws.s3.Bucket(stack, 'MyBucket', {

versioned: true,

});
```

4. AIOps (Artificial Intelligence for IT Operations)

AIOps leverages AI and machine learning to enhance IT operations. It helps in automating incident detection, root cause analysis, and remediation. By analyzing vast amounts of data from logs, metrics, and events, AIOps can proactively identify and address issues, ensuring higher system reliability.

```
# Example of anomaly detection using machine learning

if anomaly_detector.detect(data):

alert_team('Anomaly detected in server metrics.')
```

5. Serverless and Function as a Service (FaaS)

Serverless computing and FaaS platforms like AWS Lambda and Azure Functions are becoming mainstream. They offer a serverless architecture where developers focus solely on code without managing infrastructure. DevOps teams will need to adapt their practices to deploy and manage serverless applications efficiently.

// Example AWS Lambda function in Node.js

```
exports.handler = async (event) => {
```

// Lambda function logic here

```
};
```

6. DevOps for Edge Computing

As edge computing gains traction, DevOps practices will extend to manage edge devices and applications. Edge environments have unique challenges, such as limited resources and intermittent connectivity, making automation and orchestration crucial for ensuring reliability and performance.

 # Edge device configuration using Ansible

```
- name: Configure Edge Device

hosts: edge-device

tasks:

- name: Install required packages

apt:

name: "{{ item }}"

with_items:

- package1

- package2
```

7. Quantum Computing and DevOps

While still in its infancy, quantum computing holds the potential to disrupt various industries. DevOps practitioners should monitor developments in quantum computing and assess its potential implications for their organizations. Quantum-safe encryption and optimization problems are areas where quantum computing could impact DevOps.

 # Simulated quantum algorithm

from qiskit **import** QuantumCircuit, Aer, transpile, assemble

 # Quantum circuit logic here

8. DevOps for IoT (Internet of Things)

IoT devices are becoming more prevalent, and DevOps will play a crucial role in managing the software and firmware updates for these devices. Practices such as over-the-air (OTA) updates, device management, and security will be essential in IoT DevOps.

 # IoT firmware update process

def update_firmware(device_id, firmware_version):

 # Logic for updating firmware on IoT device

pass

9. Enhanced Observability and Monitoring

The need for robust observability and monitoring solutions will continue to grow. DevOps teams will adopt advanced tools and practices to gain deeper insights into application and infrastructure performance. Distributed tracing, log analytics, and AI-driven observability will become more prevalent.

 # Prometheus configuration for Kubernetes monitoring

scrape_configs:

- job_name: 'kubernetes-pods'

kubernetes_sd_configs:

- role: pod

relabel_configs:

 # Relabeling and configuration here

10. Ethical and Responsible DevOps

As technology becomes more influential, there will be an increased focus on ethical and responsible AI and DevOps practices. Organizations will need to consider the ethical implications of AI-powered decisions and ensure transparency, fairness, and accountability.

The future of DevOps is exciting and filled with possibilities. Embracing these emerging technologies and trends will be essential for organizations to stay competitive, deliver high-quality software, and meet the evolving needs of their customers. DevOps professionals should continue to learn, adapt, and innovate as they navigate this ever-evolving landscape.

Section 20.2: DevOps and the Internet of Things (IoT)

The Internet of Things (IoT) is revolutionizing how we interact with the world around us. It refers to the network of interconnected devices, sensors, and objects that collect and exchange data. These devices range from smart thermostats and wearable fitness trackers to industrial sensors and autonomous vehicles. As IoT continues to grow, it presents unique challenges and opportunities for DevOps practices.

IoT Complexity and Scale

IoT ecosystems can be incredibly complex, comprising thousands or even millions of devices spread across various locations and environments. Each device can have different hardware, software, and communication protocols. DevOps teams must grapple with this complexity when managing IoT deployments.

Over-the-Air (OTA) Updates

One of the fundamental requirements in IoT DevOps is the ability to perform Over-the-Air (OTA) updates. OTA updates allow organizations to remotely deploy new firmware or software updates to IoT devices in the field. This capability is essential for fixing security vulnerabilities, adding new features, or addressing bugs without the need for physical intervention.

 # Sample OTA update process for an IoT device

```
def perform_ota_update(device_id, new_firmware_version):
```

 # Connect to the device remotely

```
device = connect_to_device(device_id)
```

```python
# Check if the device is eligible for the update

if device.is_eligible_for_update(new_firmware_version):

# Trigger the OTA update process

device.start_ota_update(new_firmware_version)

else:

print("Device is not eligible for the update.")
```

Device Management and Monitoring

IoT DevOps also involves robust device management and monitoring practices. This includes tracking the status, health, and performance of IoT devices in real-time. Tools like device management platforms and IoT-specific monitoring solutions are crucial for ensuring the reliability and availability of IoT deployments.

Security Challenges

IoT devices are often deployed in environments where security is paramount, such as healthcare, industrial automation, and smart cities. DevOps teams must prioritize security by implementing encryption, secure boot processes, and access controls. Additionally, the ability to respond quickly to security vulnerabilities with OTA updates is essential.

```yaml
# IoT device security configuration

security:

encryption: true

secure_boot: true
```

access_controls:

- user: admin

permissions: read-write

- user: guest

permissions: read-only

Edge Computing in IoT

Edge computing is closely associated with IoT. It involves processing data closer to the source, which can reduce latency and bandwidth requirements. DevOps practices extend to managing edge computing nodes and ensuring seamless integration with cloud-based services.

 # Deploying an edge computing application with Docker Compose

docker-compose up -d

IoT-Specific DevOps Tools

The IoT landscape has given rise to specialized DevOps tools designed for managing IoT deployments. These tools often incorporate features for device management, OTA updates, and IoT-specific monitoring. DevOps professionals should evaluate and integrate these tools into their workflows.

Scalability and Flexibility

IoT environments can experience rapid scaling as new devices are added. DevOps practices should account for this scalability by employing cloud-based infrastructure and containerization to accommodate IoT growth seamlessly.

 # Scalable IoT infrastructure using Kubernetes

```
apiVersion: apps/v1

kind: Deployment

metadata:

name: iot-device-manager

spec:

replicas: 5

selector:

matchLabels:

app: iot-device-manager

template:

metadata:

labels:

app: iot-device-manager

spec:

containers:

- name: iot-device-manager

image: iot-device-manager:v1.0.0
```

Interoperability and Standards

Interoperability is a significant challenge in IoT, given the diversity of devices and protocols. DevOps teams should pay attention to emerging IoT standards and protocols that facilitate device communication and data exchange.

Data Analytics and Insights

IoT generates vast amounts of data. DevOps practices should include data analytics and insights to derive value from this data. Advanced analytics, machine learning, and AI can uncover patterns, anomalies, and opportunities for optimization.

 # IoT data analytics and visualization

import pandas **as** pd

import matplotlib.pyplot **as** plt

 # Data analysis and visualization code here

In conclusion, IoT is reshaping industries and creating new possibilities. DevOps plays a crucial role in ensuring the successful deployment, management, and security of IoT ecosystems. As organizations continue to embrace IoT technologies, DevOps professionals must adapt to the unique challenges and opportunities presented by the Internet of Things.

Section 20.3: The Convergence of DevOps and Edge Computing

Edge computing, a paradigm that involves processing data closer to its source, has gained significant traction in recent years. This approach reduces latency, improves real-time decision-making, and optimizes bandwidth usage. Edge computing and DevOps are converging to enable organizations to efficiently manage and scale edge deployments while maintaining operational excellence.

Challenges in Edge Computing

Edge computing environments are inherently diverse and distributed. They may include IoT devices, sensors, gateways, and edge servers, all serving different purposes. Managing and coordinating these components in remote or harsh environments can be challenging. DevOps practices can address these challenges.

Infrastructure as Code (IaC) for Edge

Infrastructure as Code (IaC) principles are equally applicable to edge computing. Defining and provisioning edge resources through code allows for consistency and automation. Tools like Ansible, Terraform, and Kubernetes are valuable in managing edge infrastructure.

```
# Provisioning edge infrastructure with Terraform

resource "aws_instance" "edge_server" {

ami = "ami-0c55b159cbfafe1f0"

instance_type = "t2.micro"

count = 3

tags = {

Name = "edge-server-${count.index}"

}

}
```

Continuous Integration and Deployment (CI/CD) for Edge Applications

CI/CD pipelines are extended to include edge applications and services. This enables rapid development and deployment of edge code while ensuring reliability. Testing and validation are critical to prevent issues in remote edge locations.

 # Edge application CI/CD pipeline configuration

stages:

- build

- test

- deploy_edge

- deploy_cloud

deploy_edge:

stage: deploy_edge

script:

- deploy_to_edge.sh

Monitoring and Management of Edge Devices

Real-time monitoring and management of edge devices are essential for maintaining the health and performance of edge deployments. DevOps teams use monitoring tools and remote management capabilities to detect issues and apply updates.

 # Remote monitoring and management of edge devices

ssh edge-device-01 'tail -f /var/log/application.log'

ssh edge-device-02 'update_edge_application.sh'

Edge Security and DevSecOps

Edge devices are often deployed in uncontrolled or hostile environments, making security a top concern. DevSecOps practices are crucial to address vulnerabilities, apply patches, and enforce security policies across edge devices.

 # DevSecOps pipeline for edge security

stages:

- build

- test

- scan_vulnerabilities

- apply_patches

- enforce_policies

Scaling Edge Deployments

Edge computing deployments can rapidly scale as new locations and devices are added. DevOps practices enable organizations to scale edge resources dynamically and efficiently, ensuring seamless growth.

 # Scaling edge resources with Kubernetes

kubectl scale deployment edge-application—replicas=5

Edge and Cloud Integration

Edge and cloud computing can complement each other. DevOps principles facilitate the integration of edge and cloud services, ensuring data synchronization, load balancing, and redundancy.

 # Edge-to-cloud data synchronization

if edge_data_changed():

sync_data_to_cloud()

Edge DevOps Best Practices

- **Edge-specific testing:** Conduct testing that mimics edge conditions and network constraints.

- **Edge orchestration:** Use orchestration tools like Kubernetes to manage edge containers.

- **Remote logging:** Implement centralized logging to collect and analyze edge device logs.

- **Edge backups:** Regularly backup edge configurations and data to ensure data integrity.

- **Edge-friendly deployments:** Optimize applications for resource-constrained edge devices.

In conclusion, the convergence of DevOps and edge computing empowers organizations to harness the benefits of distributed processing while maintaining operational efficiency. By applying DevOps practices to edge environments, businesses can ensure the reliability, security, and scalability of their edge deployments, driving innovation in various industries.

Section 20.4: Preparing for the Next Wave of DevOps Innovations

As the world of technology evolves at an unprecedented pace, DevOps continues to adapt and innovate to meet the ever-changing demands of software development and IT operations. In this section, we will explore some of the key trends and emerging technologies that are poised to shape the future of DevOps.

1. GitOps and Infrastructure as Code (IaC) Maturation

GitOps is an approach that leverages Git repositories as the source of truth for infrastructure and application deployment. It simplifies the management of infrastructure changes by representing them as code, making IaC even more integral to DevOps. In the future, we can expect GitOps and IaC to mature further, offering enhanced automation, security, and governance.

2. AIOps and Intelligent Automation

Artificial Intelligence for IT Operations (AIOps) is gaining prominence, using machine learning and AI algorithms to automate tasks, detect anomalies, and optimize IT operations. AIOps can revolutionize incident response, monitoring, and performance management in DevOps by providing predictive and prescriptive insights.

```
# Example of AIOps anomaly detection

if detect_anomaly():

alert_devops_team()

initiate_automatic_remediation()
```

3. Serverless and Function as a Service (FaaS)

Serverless computing and Function as a Service (FaaS) are reshaping how applications are developed and deployed. DevOps teams will need to adapt to manage serverless functions, coordinate event-driven architectures, and optimize resource usage in this serverless paradigm.

 # Serverless deployment configuration

functions:

- name: my-function

runtime: nodejs14.x

handler: index.handler

events:

- http:

path: /my-function

method: GET

4. Edge DevOps and Edge-native Applications

As discussed in Section 20.3, edge computing is on the rise. Edge DevOps will become essential for managing and scaling edge deployments. Edge-native applications will emerge, requiring specialized DevOps practices for resource-constrained, remote environments.

5. DevOps for AI and Machine Learning (MLOps)

The integration of AI and machine learning into applications will demand specialized DevOps practices known as MLOps. This includes versioning and deploying machine learning models, continuous training, and ensuring data quality in AI-driven systems.

 # MLOps pipeline for model training and deployment

stages:

- data_preparation

- model_training

- model_evaluation

- model_deployment

6. Cloud-native and Kubernetes-native DevOps

Cloud-native technologies, such as Kubernetes, are becoming the foundation of modern application development. DevOps practices are evolving to align with cloud-native principles, focusing on microservices, containers, and cloud services.

 # Kubernetes-native DevOps practices

apiVersion: apps/v1

kind: Deployment

metadata:

name: my-app

spec:

```
replicas: 3

template:

spec:

containers:

- name: my-app-container

image: my-app:latest
```

7. Quantum Computing DevOps

Although in its early stages, quantum computing holds the potential to revolutionize computing. DevOps for quantum computing will involve managing quantum algorithms, simulators, and eventually quantum hardware, presenting unique challenges and opportunities.

8. Regulatory and Compliance Automation

As data privacy and security regulations evolve, DevOps will need to integrate automated compliance checks into CI/CD pipelines. Tools and practices for regulatory compliance automation will become essential in ensuring that software deployments meet legal and industry-specific requirements.

9. DevOps for Non-Traditional IT Environments

DevOps principles will extend beyond traditional IT to industries like healthcare, finance, and manufacturing. Customized DevOps solutions will be developed to address unique challenges and compliance requirements in these sectors.

10. Ethical DevOps and Responsible AI

With the increasing use of AI and automation, ethical considerations are gaining importance. DevOps will need to incorporate practices that ensure responsible AI and ethical decision-making in software development.

In conclusion, the future of DevOps is exciting and dynamic, driven by rapid advancements in technology and evolving business needs. DevOps professionals must stay adaptable and continually update their skills to embrace these innovations and contribute to the success of their organizations in the ever-evolving landscape of software development and IT operations.

Section 20.5: Envisioning the Future of Software Development with DevOps

As we look ahead to the future of software development, it becomes evident that DevOps will continue to play a pivotal role in shaping the industry. The convergence of technology trends and the changing landscape of business requirements offer a glimpse into how software development will evolve. In this final section, we explore the vision of the future of software development empowered by DevOps practices.

1. DevOps as the New Standard

DevOps, once considered a cutting-edge approach, is poised to become the standard way of delivering software. Organizations of all sizes and across industries will embrace DevOps principles to accelerate development, enhance collaboration, and improve software quality.

2. AI-Augmented Development

Artificial intelligence (AI) will be an integral part of the development process. AI-driven tools will assist developers in writing code, identifying and fixing issues, and automating repetitive tasks, ultimately boosting productivity and efficiency.

 # AI-assisted code completion and error detection

def calculate_total_expenses(data):

if data:

return sum(data['expenses'])

return 0

3. No-Code and Low-Code Development

The rise of no-code and low-code platforms will empower business users and citizen developers to create software applications without extensive coding knowledge. DevOps will adapt to support the rapid deployment of applications built on these platforms.

4. Cloud-Native and Hybrid Architectures

Cloud-native and hybrid cloud architectures will dominate the software landscape. DevOps practices will continue to evolve to effectively manage and orchestrate applications across multiple cloud providers and on-premises environments.

 # Hybrid cloud deployment configuration

environments:

- name: aws-prod

provider: AWS

- name: azure-dev

provider: Azure

- name: on-premises

provider: On-premises

5. Decentralized and Distributed Teams

The traditional model of co-located development teams will give way to decentralized and distributed teams. DevOps tools and practices will facilitate seamless collaboration among team members across different geographical locations.

6. Continuous Everything

The concept of "continuous" will extend beyond CI/CD to include continuous testing, continuous security, and continuous compliance. DevOps pipelines will become more comprehensive, ensuring that every aspect of software development is continuously monitored and improved.

7. DevOps for IoT and Edge Computing

As the Internet of Things (IoT) and edge computing gain prominence, DevOps will adapt to support the unique challenges of these domains. Managing edge devices, deploying updates, and ensuring reliability will become key focus areas.

```
# DevOps for edge device deployment

if deploy_to_edge_device():

monitor_device_health()
```

update_device_firmware()

8. Enhanced Security Integration

Security will be integrated at every stage of the development process. DevSecOps practices will be ingrained in DevOps, with security checks and vulnerability assessments seamlessly integrated into CI/CD pipelines.

9. User-Centric Development

User experience (UX) and user feedback will drive development decisions. DevOps teams will prioritize user-centric design and development practices, leveraging data and feedback to continually improve applications.

10. Sustainable and Responsible Development

Sustainability and ethical considerations will become integral to software development. DevOps will include practices that assess and minimize the environmental impact of software, as well as ensure responsible and ethical AI and automation.

In this envisioned future, DevOps will not only be a methodology but a way of life for software professionals. It will continuously adapt to harness emerging technologies, meet evolving business demands, and uphold the principles of collaboration, automation, and quality that define the DevOps movement. As software development evolves, DevOps will remain at the forefront, guiding the industry toward a future of innovation and excellence.

Printed in the USA
CPSIA information can be obtained
at www.ICGtesting.com
CBHW031525101024
15669CB00034B/308